GIVE YOUR LIFE A
SUCCESS
MAKE
OVER

Wes Beavis

POWERBORN

Give Your Life a Success Makeover
by Wes Beavis

Copyright ©2004 W. J. Beavis

1st printing April 2004
3rd printing October 2004

PRINTED IN THE UNITED STATES OF AMERICA BY
Delta Printing Solutions
Valencia, CA

DESIGN AND LAYOUT BY
PlainJoeStudios.com

COPYRIGHT & PUBLISHING ADMINISTRATION BY
POWERBORN
631 Via Paraiso
Corona, California USA 92882
Phone (951) 739-0634
Fax (714) 464-4171
www.WesBeavis.com

Beavis, Wesley James, 1962-
    Give Your Life a Success Makeover / Wes Beavis
        p.   cm.
    ISBN 1–888741–04–X
    1. Success—United States.   2. Quality of life—
United States.   3. Leadership—United States.
    4. Self-actualization / Maturation (Psychology)   I. Title
        158.1 BEA —dc20   2004

9 8 7 6 5 4 3

Also by the author:

Become the Person You Dream of Being

Dating the Dream: Building a Winning Relationship with Your Desires

Escape to Prosperity

Dedicated to the loves of my life. . .

Ellie and our sons, David & Zachary

Contents

Introduction

I n recent years, we have seen the emergence of 'The Makeover' in television programming. It is the practice of taking a person, in whatever shape they are in, and making them better. Sometimes this is as simple as taking the person backstage where they are treated to some new clothes and a new hairstyle. To see a person go from glum to glamorous is always entertaining and even inspiring.

Over time, the makeover concept has evolved. We now have the 'Extreme Makeover'. And dare I say, I love it! The producers of the show remove selected individuals from their life setting (family, town, work) for up to three months. During this time, all types of plastic surgeons, laser eye surgeons and dentists go to work on them. Using marvelously invasive surgical procedures, they improve the physical features of their patients. For days after the surgery, the makeover recipients look like they've been run over by a convoy of cattle trucks. Yet as healing takes place, the 'new self' starts to take shape. From there it's off to the gym for six weeks of intensive workouts with a personal trainer. With a better diet, better clothes and better hair, they are then re-introduced to their previous life setting. In short, they are brought back better than what they were before.

> Is it possible that you have become shackled to a previous success?

Sure, they don't come back perfect. And neither does life become perfect just because they have a new nose, white teeth and a 'refreshed' look. Yet, the simple fact is that they have improved on what they were before. A new energy abounds. Along with their renewed appearance, there is a renewed optimism for the future. Life got better because improvement took place. That is the spirit of the Success Makeover. Our whole life gets better as a result of improving.

It is quite possible that you have already

made your life better than average. Compared to others, you are considered successful. But it is also possible that you are stuck. That whilst you have achieved 'better than average' status, you have advanced no further. The reality is that even a successful life loses its luster without further advances being on the horizon.

Perhaps you were content upon reaching a certain level of success and thought that the contentment would last. Maybe you took a peek at what was required to take the next step but decided to rest a while, and you have been resting ever since. Is it possible that you have become shackled to a previous success? Something has enticed you to read this book. Could it be that you miss the excitement that comes with seeing yourself improve? Could it be that you 'arrived' long ago and now you miss the thrill of the challenge? You are ready to give your life a success makeover. Let's go for it!

Wes Beavis

CHAPTER I

Refresh Your Success

I was asked recently, "What is your definition of success?" I have spent many years contemplating the idea of being successful. In my quest to discover success, I have been college educated, traveled around the world, married a beautiful woman, fathered a wonderful family, owned property free and clear, owned luxury vehicles, boats and motorcycles, fostered a healthy body, cultivated lifelong friendships, and helped humanitarian organizations. All of these are wonderful accomplishments but none define success. They are the fruits of success.

My conclusion is that success is not a specific achievement, level or possession. It is an orientation. Success is finishing today having improved on yesterday and doing the same tomorrow. Anyone who gears their life according to this definition will enjoy the delightful fruits of success.

But even the sweetest fruits of our hard earned success can lose their ability to add zest and flavor to our lives. As much as we deserve to savor the current harvest, the fruits of success will only nourish us for a season. To keep our success fresh, we need to move into new territory. Success beckons us to advance.

The Success Slump

Preparing delicious meals is a skill. Admittedly, my interest has been more directed towards the eating process. Then came a day in my life when I decided to increase my competence in meal preparation. We had never owned an outdoor grill. Since it was the middle of summer, I thought buying one would be a good place to start the development of my culinary skills. After years of not having the vaguest interest in things of the kitchen, I decided to buy a six hundred dollar barbeque. A typical

> Success is finishing today having improved on yesterday and doing the same tomorrow.

male approach! My patient wife, Ellie, reminded me that, had the grill been her idea, I would have convinced her that the kitchen stove with the windows open would have sufficed! Not wanting to deter my new found enthusiasm, however, she didn't rub it in.

So I headed down to the city market place. Located there was a store that specialized exclusively in outdoor grills. It was part of a successful chain of multi-national stores. They were well set up with many styles and models. Having spent some time examining the options, I made my decision. In talking with the salesman, I asked whether there was any room for negotiation on the price. Experience has taught me to inquire just in case a discount is there for the asking. Unfortunately, the salesman responded by saying, "All of the prices are set by our head office so we can't give any discounts." I paid the full price for the barbeque plus a little extra to have them assemble the unit. The plan was for me to return the next day to pick it up.

The next afternoon, I arrived at the store. After submitting my purchase documents to the clerk at the front of the store, I asked to see the assembled unit. It seemed prudent for me to check, prior to driving my van around to the loading dock, that it was the right model. Following the clerk through to the storeroom, it wasn't long before I realized that the grill was missing.

The storeroom was full of boxes and other items but my grill was no where to be seen. Moments later, the clerk said, "Oh, we put it in there," pointing to a closed door. I looked at the sign on the door and replied, "But that's the restroom!" I thought he was playing a practical joke on me, but he wasn't. He explained that they often put assembled units in the restroom when the storage area got too cluttered. He tried to open the door only to discover that someone was using the facility. So the clerk asked me to wait. This proved to be a mistake.

I wandered through the store to help pass the time and in doing so, I had time to think about what had transpired. Why was I buying a six hundred dollar food preparation appliance out of a toilet? The more I pondered it, the more it became an irksome thought to me. About fifteen minutes had passed by, yet no one had emerged from the restroom where my barbeque was being held hostage. So I returned to the store clerk and expressed my apprehensions.

The store clerk laughed it off as if it was no big deal. Yet, in my mind, it was becoming a bigger deal than what he realized. Other salesmen in the store were coming over to join what was the only action in the store at the time. Eventually, after making no headway with the sales team, I asked the all-important question: "May I speak to the store manager?" The clerk stammered somewhat and then said, "He's not here at the moment." I asked, "Why not?" To which he sheepishly replied, "Because he's the one in the restroom!"

When the manager finally emerged, I told him my psychological predicament. As a child, I had been taught never to take food or drink into a restroom. How could I cook meals on a grill that I had purchased

> Why was I buying a six hundred dollar food preparation appliance out of a toilet?

out of one? Resting on the laurels of his company's success and reputation, the manager seemed unperturbed by my angst. He tried to convince me that my thinking was erroneous. Without saying a word, I took my credit card from my wallet and laid it on the counter. He knew exactly what was about to go down. I requested a refund.

Displaying a fine example to his sales team, the manager reversed his previous position. He offered me the floor model, a huge discount and a good apology. In doing so, he retained my customer loyalty and regained the store's successful edge. For a few moments, they had lost their edge and were going backwards. For a few moments, they were mired in a success slump.

Forward Motion

Microsoft's chairman and chief executive officer, Bill Gates, once said, "The hardest thing to overcome is your initial success." Anyone who has succeeded enough to experience a level of comfort will agree. While going from ground floor obscurity to success is difficult enough, going from success to greater success is even more difficult.

There is every possibility that you may be experiencing a success slump; that you are stuck, mired, fixated to the honored position of a previous achievement. It's a vulnerable position to be in. Like the outdoor grill store, your success can blind you from seeing that you're losing your edge. And losing your edge will cause you to slip backwards.

> "A man without a future is bound to return to his past."
>
> A.R. Bernard

Rarely does anyone lose their edge by choice. Going backwards is never an intention. Going backwards is what happens when you don't have a goal to call you forward. When a convict escapes from a maximum security prison, the authorities have a specific strategy for recapturing the fugitive. They know that there is a tendency for fugitives to go back to previous 'hangouts' and re-connect with previous relationships. So while law enforcement will spend some time tracking the trail of the fugitive, they will also 'stake out' all the places and people with whom the fugitive was connected prior to incarceration. A.R. Bernard sums up this tendency of human nature by saying, "A man without a future is bound to return to his past."

There is one thing that sharks and people have in common. The need to be moving forward. For sharks, forward motion is the only way for them to extract life giving oxygen from their environment. For humans, forward motion is what stops them from succumbing to life draining stagnation. Studying the characteristics of success from a scientific standpoint, Dr. David Niven draws this conclusion: "People need to keep moving forward in order for their dreams to live. You don't need to do everything today, but you do need to do something every day. Those who do not feel they are taking steps towards their goals are five times more likely to give up and three times less likely to feel satisfied with their lives."

Of all the things that can hold us back, our previous success can be the biggest culprit. We never intend it to be, but this is how it happens. When we are on the ground floor of life and want to rise above it, we stretch, toil and sweat our way into a better position. Upon achieving that better position, we're understandably weary. So we camp out at that place. Too easily what we intended to be a temporary place of rest and re-creation, becomes a place of permanent residency. Unless we are beckoned by a new vision for our future, we end up staying put. And as we do, future expanding opportunities are passing us by.

No current success is worth denying you the joy of future victory. The first thing that you will discover when you boldly step in the direction of a future dream, is that the step may often be backwards. For example, financial liberation often requires people to take a step backwards in lifestyle in order to set themselves on a course for future prosperity. Many times, your advancement requires you to step down in order to step higher. For this reason, some find themselves mired in a success slump. Not wanting to lose any ground causes them to stay put with what they've got. And that's what they end up with—what they've already got.

Why does the one step back, two steps forward

process typify the improvement journey? Perhaps it's part of the pride eradicating process demanded by the next level. Perhaps it is to reserve the spoils for those who are willing to pay the price. Regardless, we would do well to heed what French novelist,

> **Of all the things that can hold us back, our previous success can be the biggest culprit.**

Andre Gide, said, "One does not discover new lands without consenting to lose sight of the shore for a very long time."

Success is about moving forward. It is about discovering new lands, new opportunities and new experiences. It is about bidding farewell to a current position in order to advance to an improved position. We are designed for forward motion. To grow, to produce and to expand your positive influence is your way forward. It is the remedy to a success slump. And it is the key to a success makeover.

CHAPTER 2

Turning Up Your Vision Thermostat

After years as a motivational speaker, I have come to this conclusion. No one can advance beyond the vision that they have for their own life. It doesn't matter how much potential you have, how beautiful you appear in someone else's eyes, or how much opportunity surrounds you, if you can't see it, you will never be it.

Someone may have the most glorious vision for your life. They could share it with you at a nice restaurant. They could put the vision in a song and sing it to you in the candlelight. They could hop on the restaurant table and preach it to you until they are sure you 'get it'. They could recite it in a poem, get Aunt Bessie to come in with the Hallelujah Gospel Choir and wail it, or they could simply say it with flowers. But your life will remain unchanged unless you develop your own vision for it. Someone else's vision for your life may be awesome but it's not enough. No matter how much a friend may believe that you

> You cannot advance beyond the vision that your have for your own life.

belong there, unless you can first see yourself in a better place, you will never experience that better place. You cannot advance beyond the vision that you have for your own life.

My wife, Ellie, knows that when I am working on a writing project, I much prefer leaving our home in the city and driving up to our home in the mountains. There is something about the air and atmosphere at seven thousand feet that lends itself to being able to focus thoughts. But being at this altitude during the winter months means that my first task upon arrival is to turn up the thermostat for the central heating. Without such heat, my fingers would freeze in the time it takes me to hunt and peck my way around the keyboard. I set the thermostat to raise the room temperature, knowing that unless I do so, the temperature of our mountain home will stay the same.

The same principle applies to our lives. Unless we raise our vision, we are predetermined to stay the same. To raise the quality of our life, we must first establish in our mind a vision for living life at that improved level. Even though others may try to help us visualize a better life, ultimately we rise or fall to the level of the 'me I see'. As philosopher William James said, "We grow as far as our self-image." It is impossible to advance beyond the perception we have of ourselves. We cannot lead ourselves somewhere that we have not yet been in our minds. As important as it is to have a vision for your future, it is even more

> **Without being guided by a vision, momentum can actually smash you into a state of going nowhere.**

important for you to have a clear picture of what YOU will look like in the future.

Success creates momentum. And momentum is extremely helpful in moving you forward. But momentum created by your previous achievements can only get you so far. Without being guided by a vision, momentum can actually smash you into a state of going nowhere. I have seen successful people shut down tremendous success momentum because they couldn't picture themselves living beyond their current position. For lack of a vision, their momentum stalled with their life following suit.

There is another characteristic of the heating thermostat that applies to the subject of elevating the quality of our lives. Once you set the thermostat to a certain temperature level, it takes time for the heater to warm the room up to that temperature. The same can be said of setting a new vision for your life. It's going to take time, perhaps even years, for your life to rise to the level of the vision that you have set. There is a time delay between setting the vision and fulfilling the vision. What happens during this time delay? A lot of hard work!

> Some have set their vision thermostat high, only to lower it at every point of failure or discouragement. The end result is they keep lowering their vision until it matches what they already have.

When our boys were little, they would use our outdoor Jacuzzi as a makeshift swimming pool. This sufficed for a few years until they outgrew it, so we re-developed the backyard to include a pool. Though they had a lot of fun in that Jacuzzi, Ellie and I decided that we should make it available for another family to enjoy. So as I was placing an advertisement in the local paper, I decided to also place an ad for an exercise treadmill which, embarrassingly I must confess, we weren't using.

The following week, we received forty phone calls

> We are not human versions of wildebeests—always moving on, but heading to nowhere special.

from people wanting the Jacuzzi. Yet, not one serious expression of interest was received for the exercise machine. I concluded that more people had a vision for relaxing in a hot tub than for sweating it out on the treadmill. I could say that the treadmill would have done them more good but then, that would be slightly hypocritical of me, wouldn't it?

Without a doubt, having a vision for a better life does set you on a course of hard work. This is usually the reason why many prefer not to get into the vision business in the first place. The time between setting the vision and having the vision become reality is, quite frankly, filled with challenges. It is human nature to come up with an excuse rather than come up with the effort. That's why you see more people living to the level of their excuses rather than the level of their potential. Author Eddie Windsor sums it up well saying, "Next to hardness, you will find excuseness!"

Not everyone who lacks a vision for their life is that way because they lack a work ethic. Some have set their vision thermostat high, only to lower it at every point of failure or discouragement. The end result is they keep lowering their vision until it matches what they already have. You know what I'm saying because you may have done the same. The heartbreaks of having reality fall short of expectation time and time again lead you to wonder whether you may have aimed too high. You make adjustments which usually entail rationalizing your dreams downward. For instance, you may have dreamed of celebrating your wedding anniversary by taking your wife to Paris for a week, but after several setbacks, you settle for taking her to the local movie theater for a matinee!

Understand that the purpose in setting a vision for your life is not to set you up for disappointment, but rather to set you towards increase. Leadership strategists, Warren Bennis & Burt Nanus, define vision as "a mental model of a desirable, realistic, future state which presently does not exist." Note their use of the word realistic. Some people's vision for the future is not realistic. Failure comes quickly and they conclude that they must not be meant to have a better life. They anesthetize their yearning for something greater and convince themselves to be content with the normalcy of their lives. But not you!

You have not relegated yourself to a life of normalcy. On the contrary, hard work is something with which you are well acquainted. As a result of having a vision, you already enjoy an above average life. While congratulations are in order, there comes a time in the pilgrimage of every successful person when you must lift up the eyes of your spirit and establish a new vision for yourself: A vision of an improved position from where you are now.

A life of increased value is largely the result of our decisions— what we say yes to and what we say no to. Having a strong vision helps us to decide when it's right to say yes and when it's right to say no. A strong vision for the future helps successful people from sabotaging their success.

> Improvement comes, more often than not, by way of the treadmill, not the hot-tub!

Recently I heard Jentzen Franklin implore a group of leaders to resist the temptation to trade in their fighting spirit for a civilian spirit. He used King David as an example of a man who went through a season of easing up as a warrior. Instead of fulfilling his role as a leader, he let others do it as he adopted a civilian life. While his army was gaining new territory and land, King David was losing something far more valuable. He was losing his integrity. A vision for improving one's position is so valuable to a warrior. At the very least, it reduces the potential that a warrior will sabotage the success they have already attained.

By all means, enjoy the level of comfort you have earned, but don't let it stop you from discovering your more valuable self. Life gets better for those who envision it better. We are not human versions of wildebeests—always moving on, but heading to nowhere special. What is ahead of you is very special. The success you have known is only a fraction of what lies ahead. Don't let anyone or anything cause you to think that your best days are behind you.

Having evaluated the claims and experiences of success for many years, I have come to this simple conclusion: Future success comes by way of daily improvement. And improvement comes, more often than not, by way of the treadmill, not the hot-tub. When your vision for the future is exciting, you are energized to pay the price of the necessary treadmill time!

Envisioning a better future requires clear thinking and room for spontaneous ideas to surface. This happens best in an environment of solitude. Yet, too often, this is where we short-change ourselves. We are so busy presiding over our current achievements, blessings and challenges, that we don't give our minds the necessary space to creatively breathe.

Give yourself the benefit of quality time in an uplifting environment. Draw aside from others and your usual activities. This is easier said than done so you are advised to actually plan for it. Go somewhere by yourself, solely for the purpose of dreaming about you in the future. To spend a day for this purpose is far from a frivolous use of your time. If all you can manage is one afternoon, it is still worth it.

It is easier to turn up your vision thermostat if you put yourself in the right environment. Fresh visions and ideas to increase your future grow out of refreshing times and places. This is the first practical step in your success makeover.

CHAPTER 3

Be Tough With Your Emotions

One day, while playing a board game with my son, Zack, I caught an alarming glimpse of myself. We were playing a game of *Chutes and Ladders*. The premise of the game is simple: You roll the dice and work your way up to the top of the board. If the square upon which you landed had a ladder, it meant that you would ascend many rows putting you way ahead of the other player. However, if the roll of the dice landed you on a square with a chute, the opposite would happen. You would descend many rows causing you to lose any recent advances. The game could be easily re-named, *Welcome to Life!*

It was the first time Zack had played the game. He was doing well. Clobbering his Dad with some fortunate high rolls of the dice and landing on a ladder or two, he was loving the game until he landed on a chute. As I moved his board piece to the square to which the chute had descended, Zack gave me a perplexed look. When it finally sank in that this was part of the game, he became

> If only attitudes and emotions had the same stability and dependability of concrete. That once we got the right attitude laid in our mind, it would forever stay there.

stricken with grief. Up to that point Zack was so enjoying the feelings of victory but upon experiencing a setback, he became unglued emotionally.

What had started out to be fun had turned into torment for Zack. The feelings that heightened the exhilaration when everything was going right, flipped to become feelings that deepened the despair when things went wrong. It was alarming. But not because the game, which was meant to be a fun activity, went sour. It was alarming because I could see so much of myself in my six year old's response! How many times had I responded the same way to life's setbacks?

In my motivational seminars, I talk about my

love of concrete. The reason for my enthusiasm is because once you mix it and set it, you can forget it. When Ellie and I commissioned builders to build our first home, the construction of the driveway and pathway to the front door was not included in the building contract. We were young and significantly tight on financial solvency. Getting the funds to build the house was task enough. Consideration for the concrete driveway and pathway was way down the list. We concluded that these could come later.

> A successful person, just as much as anyone, needs to improve their ability to be positive.

Soon after we moved into the new home, we had a season of torrential rains. The deluge turned the hard, clay ground of our front yard into the sloppiest mud mess imaginable. We made a makeshift pathway out of timber boards. The boards worked for a little while, until the oozing clay gobbled them up. We kept laying new boards over them, each time lamenting the insolvency which had put us in this sloppy mess.

We were relieved when we could afford to have a concrete driveway and pathway constructed. Once the concrete was laid and had a chance to harden, we never had to worry about the mud again. More rains would come, but the concrete stayed put, unaffected by the torrents of water which simply drained away.

If only attitudes and emotions had the same stability and dependability of concrete. That once we got the right attitude laid in our mind, it would forever stay there. That once we dealt with an emotion, it would never raise its destabilizing head again. The reality is that attitudes and emotions are like timber boards laid over sloppy clay. You have to be ever mindful of them and attending to them, lest they get swallowed up by the inevitable mud of life.

An attitude or emotion is no respecter of a person's lofty position. A good disposition can get a person to great heights, but a person at great heights is not immune to slipping into a regrettable disposition. I have caved into a negative attitude more than I care to admit. Even though I have attained a life that many others wish they had, there are still days when I take on the attitude of an ungrateful jerk.

The fact is that a successful person, just as much as anyone, needs to improve their ability to be positive. They may even need it more because the journey can often leave a successful person with more fodder for cynicism and pessimism than the average Joe. Successful people may experience more heartache, disappointment, self-doubt, jealousy, and criticism than most. All of that puts the successful person, as with any other person, in need of an attitude makeover from time to time.

The Path to Mastery

There is a pathway to success. This pathway never changes, regardless of whether your goal is to learn to play the guitar or build a multi-million dollar enterprise. While choosing a positive attitude is essential to moving along the pathway, understanding the pathway will make it easier to keep a positive attitude engaged. My brother, Cameron, has mapped the pathway into what he calls *The Path to Mastery*.

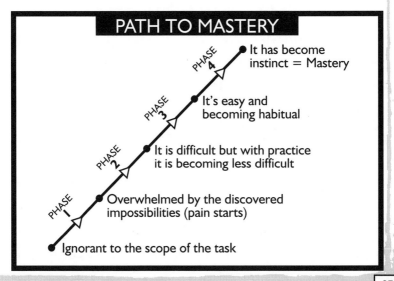

PATH TO MASTERY

PHASE 4 — It has become instinct = Mastery

PHASE 3 — It's easy and becoming habitual

PHASE 2 — It is difficult but with practice it is becoming less difficult

PHASE 1 — Overwhelmed by the discovered impossibilities (pain starts)

Ignorant to the scope of the task

According to this diagram, the starting point is a place of ignorance to the scope of the task; a place where ignorance is bliss. Phase 1 is the process of moving from this bliss to being overwhelmed by the discovered impossibilities of the task. From this painful phase, the pathway moves towards an understanding that while the task is difficult, practice increases skill which reduces difficulty. In Phase 4, the pathway continues the trajectory from difficulty to ease as the task becomes habitual. Finally, the task becomes instinctive and mastered.

This is the pathway that you travel regardless of the type of advancement for which you desire. Whether you are starting to sell products, starting an organization, or commencing a fitness program, the pathway to mastery has stages. When you understand the nuances of each stage, and acknowledge that you are not just bouncing around for no rhyme or reason, you are more able to stay positive and deal with your emotions.

You Are Paid to be Positive

A friend of mine is the president of a multi-million dollar, non-profit organization. To finance a major expansion program, he conducted a fund raising campaign. The goal was to raise eight million dollars. At the conclusion of the campaign, only six million dollars was raised. It was certainly a perspective test. Do you celebrate the fact that six million dollars was brought to a previously barren table? Or do you bemoan the fact that the table was still two million dollars short?

Six months later, I asked my friend how he personally dealt with the issue. Regardless of the fact that they had raised a huge amount of capital, he still had to deal with a financial dilemma of how to cover the two million dollar shortfall. His answer was simple: "At the end of the day, we are paid to be positive."

There is nothing gained from discouragement. No one is going to pay you to distribute your despair and negative meditations. Be tough with the emotions that accompany your disappointments. They will not lead you down the road to profit.

Do Not Cooperate With a Negative Spirit

The world is a mixture of adversity and opportunity. And sometimes, the adversities will get the better of us causing negative thoughts to overwhelm our mind. At this point, it is decision time. Do I cooperate with this negative spirit? Or do I refuse to cooperate with it and fight it? You and I know from experience that it is easier to cooperate with a destructive thought. You just relax into it and it will do all the work. It's like an ocean riptide. Hand yourself over to it and it will carry you right out to sea!

How do you fight a negative spirit that wants your cooperation? You do the opposite of how you feel. If you feel like withdrawing from people, you do the opposite and seek out the company of positive people. If you feel like sulking, do the opposite and start praising and encouraging others. If you feel like a failure, act like a

> Do the opposite of everything that your depressed feeling wants you to do.

success. If you feel like being depressed, do the opposite of everything that your depressed feeling wants you to do.

Sir Edmund Hillary, the New Zealand mountaineer and conqueror of Mount Everest, said, "It's not the mountain that we conquer, but ourselves." Most people are not defeated by the immensity of a task but rather they are defeated by their own thinking.

How to Assess Yourself

When positive results are not there when you need them, do not assess yourself by how you feel. Though emotions are your best friend when things are going well, they are your worst enemy when setbacks occur. When you are discouraged, your emotions will lead you away from the truth rather than draw you towards it. According to Elias L. Magoon, our worth should always be determined by our good deeds, rather than the emotions that we feel.

> **When you are down, your emotions will lead you away from the truth rather than towards it.**

When in a discouraged condition, we tend to compare ourselves with others who happen to be on a winning streak. We compare ourselves at our worst, with someone else at their best. This is not a logical comparison, let alone a fair one. But when we are being guided by our emotions, logic rarely gets the opportunity to re-calibrate our flailing spirit.

Turning It Around

Viacom Chairman, Sumner Redstone, once said, "Big success is not built on success. It's built on failure, disaster and catastrophe. It's about learning to turn it around." The first step to turning around a bleak situation is to take charge over your emotions and re-establish optimism as your default attitude position.

Favor does not rest on people who are gentle with their emotions. Remain faithful to the principles of success even when you are not firing on all cylinders. It's the quickest way to getting all your cylinders firing again. Conversely, the slowest way to get back on top is to be governed by your emotions.

Be tough with your attitudes and emotions. It is a daily requirement to make adjustments. Society is very good at dwelling on and distributing the negative and it's almost impossible to escape it. The adjustments that you made to your attitudes and emotions yesterday are likely not sufficient to carry you through today. Remember that you have as much ability to 'set and forget' attitudes and emotions as you do nailing water to a wall. No matter how much success you have already experienced, your positive disposition still needs constant monitoring and refreshment.

> It's the quickest way to getting all your cylinders firing again.

Favor flows to the positive. So master your emotions.

CHAPTER 4

Get Yourself a Stronger Spirit

C aptain Kyle Kerekffy is a corporate jet pilot and a friend. On one occasion, Kyle flew some business partners and me to Utah. The purpose of our trip was to examine some corporate property which had been damaged in a storm. We spent the day starting the assessment and repair process. By the time we re-boarded the plane for our trip back to California, we were feeling good about a productive day. As we streamed our way through the air, I was delighting in the fact that it was a smooth flight. Having traveled in various aircraft, I have come to the conclusion that the smaller the aircraft, the more you feel the effects of turbulence. A Boeing 747 tends to fly steadily with an occasional buffeting around from time to time. A small aircraft can be quite the opposite—continual buffeting around with the occasional period of steadiness.

Though our flight had been calm, the final leg of the journey involved flying over the San Bernardino Mountains. From previous experience, I knew that mountain ranges come accompanied with updrafts and unpredictable wind patterns. A few pilot friends of mine had flown the mountains of Papua New Guinea. They testify to the treachery of updrafts. A fact reinforced by losing one of my friends to those mountains. So I was not oblivious to what happens when you fly a compact aircraft over mountains. We were bound to have some turbulence, but I had prepared myself.

> **Moments later, the plane morphed into a roller coaster.**

As we made our way over the peaks, I began to think that my mental preparation was not needed. The turbulence was surprisingly minor, a few bumps and that was it. With my confidence bolstered and speaking loud enough for my partners to hear me, I jested to the wind gods, "C'mon is that all you've got to throw at us?" Well, with such vocalized disrespect, I must have ticked off the wind gods, good and proper. Moments later, the plane morphed into a roller coaster.

We hit turbulence of the magnitude I had never before experienced. For the next forty minutes we churned, dropped, shook, and though we wanted it to lighten up, it never did. Making matters worse, we were instructed by air traffic control to delay our descent. In order to accommodate the windy conditions and the flight paths of larger aircraft, they vectored us

> He was calmness personified, a spirit of certainty in uncertain conditions, a veritable John Wayne of aviation.

all over the place. It felt like air traffic control was saying, "Stay up there until we call you for dinner!" Needless to say, I was praying that famous prayer: "God, if you just get me through this, I promise I will. . . !"

We finally landed. I was torn between what to do first—kiss the ground or hug the pilot. When we had retrieved our gear from the plane, Captain Kyle shook our hands and climbed behind the plane's controls. He gained clearance for take-off and headed straight up into the same turbulent air from which we had just descended. Seeing Kyle steer the plane towards his home in San Diego, I reflected on his demeanor. He made it look easy. He was calmness personified, a spirit of certainty in uncertain conditions, a veritable John Wayne of aviation. I remember thinking, 'From where do you get that strength?' And in that moment, standing on the airfield I was reminded of the answer: You get that strength from going through turbulence time after time after time.

No doubt you have made the passage through times of turbulence in getting to where you are today. Persevering through times of uncertainty and challenge to achieve your goal, has developed a strong spirit within you. But your strength and resolve must increase if you want to keep advancing. Every personal advancement requires that you develop a stronger spirit. The fortitude that got you this far may be sufficient to get you started on the next improvement. But it will be pushed beyond its limit. A stronger spirit will be needed.

> **Every personal advancement requires that you develop a stronger spirit.**

How do you get a stronger spirit? Here are some of the components that will develop it within you.

1) Push through the turbulence.

The pathway to getting ahead is hard. You'll rarely hear this message in our 'We make it easy for you!' saturated culture. Improving your life is demanding regardless of what stage of success or life that you are at. Be assured, if someone is telling you that it's easy to improve your life, look down. It's quite likely that you will find their hand is in your pocket. No one that truly cares for the vitality of your future will ever try to sell you with the notion that advancement

> Some aspects of our character and reasoning are defective and have no place in our better future.

is easy. Too many people buy Mr. Fly By Night's message that success is eeeeeasy! Then they quit at the inevitable first juncture of difficulty. You see them give up on improving their life because it turned out to be harder than they were sold to believe.

The best thing that we can tell others and tell ourselves is the truth about advancing: "Ladies and Gentlemen, this is your Captain speaking. On our flight to where we are headed, we are going to experience some turbulence. Getting through it will be uncomfortable, but we will get through it and the destination will make the effort worthwhile." After years in the life improvement business, I have concluded that positive honesty is the most productive policy.

Any personal improvement requires us to press through the 'turbulent zone'. You know you are flying through the turbulent zone when things aren't working out the way you previously imagined; when you discover that it's going to take longer than you had planned; when you see things go wrong and your emotions get bounced around; when you realize that you weren't as prepared as you thought, and when your cocksure ignorance turns into humble uncertainty. The turbulent zone is where reality and disappointment shakes the pride and hubris out of you.

> "Keep doing the right things over and over again and eventually, you will succeed."
>
> Marguerite Reeve

It doesn't sound very appealing does it? Let's face it, if fun is what you're after, the turbulent zone is not where you go for enjoyment. But the people who keep advancing to greater levels of abundance find their peace amidst the bumps.

They know that passing through the turbulent zone causes them to grow a bigger set of wings with an accompanying stronger spirit. Everyone who presses through the turbulence, rather than backing away from it, comes out on the other side endowed with admired benefits. Precondition yourself to push through the turbulence. It is a key ingredient to the success makeover.

2) Submit to the sifting mill.

If you have ambition, you will be sifted. The process of advancement will take you and drop you as grist into the mill of life. Once there, you will be grated and ground. The intensity and duration of the sifting varies from person to person, but guaranteed, no one makes it through the sifting process without having parts of them sifted out. Why? Because some aspects of our character and reasoning are defective and have no place in our better future. If allowed to stay in our lives, they would surely sabotage our gains.

Being sifted is not fun. Most people avoid the sifting mill. Why they run and hide is understandable. Who would purposely submit to something that is a threat to their comfort? Sounds reasonable enough until we remind ourselves that success never grows out of comfort. Success grows out of personal advancement and increase which comes from enduring the grind. People who purposely sacrifice current comfort do so because they see a bigger benefit ahead.

If you submit to the sifting mill and hang in there long enough, you will discover that a finer quality of you will emerge. When you assess the 'improved you', you'll realize that the sifting process, though difficult, has made you better than you were before. You will like the new version of you. In fact, you will wonder how you were ever satisfied living life as the 'pre-sifted' version.

3) Do the right things consistently.

Anyone who has gone on a long road trip with kids in the back seat are familiar with the question: "Are we there yet?" Adults tyrannize themselves with the same mindset when it comes to their goals, marriages and businesses, thinking 'Surely we should be there by now!' While setting a time frame for achieving goals helps us to overcome procrastination, too many people get crushed under the weight of thinking that they can 'hurry up' their success.

> Consistency will eventually get you to a better place.

Live with the understanding that while a vision for advancement can come quickly, achieving the advancement will always take much longer than you think. Time on the success clock passes more slowly. You can try to rush it, though more often than not, we are forced to submit to its pace. Acknowledging that it's going to take longer to advance than we initially thought is to avoid useless anxiety. Success often requires us first to be pushed to our wit's end. It is a part of the strengthening of our spirit. For our wit's end is also our wisdom's beginning in whatever area we are being challenged.

Process your way forward. Seek to improve a little every day. Apply what John C. Maxwell says, "Do something an hour a day and after five years, you'll be an expert." Apply the advice of Marguerite Reeve, wife and partner to Dr. Jim Reeve, "Keep doing the right things over and over again and eventually, you will succeed."

So many people are doing the right things but they don't do them long enough. They end up quitting because they were comparing themselves to the timing of someone else's success. Our thinking is that if someone else baked a cake in a certain amount of time, then I should be able to do the same. So we try to speed up the baking of our cake by overheating the oven temperature, whilst ignoring the fact that we are all working with different ingredients in our cake mix.

Every person's journey has its own rhythm. Be a fixture to the beat of your own process. In the hope of a quick breakthrough, many end up darting from one place to another. Doing so often produces the opposite result. Instead of a quick breakthrough, they delay their breakthrough. The answer to the timing of your success is to stay in your own lane and stay there for long enough for the desired results to come. Consistency will eventually get you to a better place.

4) Maintain your fighting stance.

When investment magnate, Warren Buffett, was asked whether he ever gives up on a stock, he answered, "We almost never sell. When we do, it's because there's something we can't fix."

The process of transitioning to a better place in life will weary you. It is tiring and we can't be faulted for desiring some respite. But too many, in their quest for a little respite, actually hang up the gloves. What eventuates is that when they get their energy back, they find they've lost their position and momentum in the journey forward. If you are stalled on the road, ask yourself: "Is this because I am in need of repair or is this because something can't be fixed?" If something can't be fixed, then even Warren Buffett calls it a day. Or as a friend of mine says, "When your horse is dead, dismount!"

Most times, however, our situation is not a case of something being irreparably broken. Often we are stalled not because 'it can't be fixed', but because we are weary, inspirationally dry or bored. For your success' sake, don't let tiredness, boredom or any other thing that can be fixed bump you off the road to eventual reward.

> If you are stalled on the road, ask yourself:
> "Is this because I am in need of repair or is this because something can't be fixed?"

When you are having problems, all you need to do is stay upright. If you opt to keep standing instead of giving up, the place where you bravely stand will be the place from which you speak with strength and authority.

Years ago, there was a popular toy called Weebles. The catch phrase for advertising these action toys was: "Weebles wobble but they don't fall down!" Advancing into new personal territory will cause you to wobble from time to time. It's just the nature of the process. Make a decision to maintain your fighting stance. Sometimes, and maybe oftentimes, things will look impossible. But if you stay upright, you will be there when the conditions change to your favor. Normally, pigs cannot fly. But when conditions change from light winds to a hurricane, even pigs can take to the skies.

Don't spend your life chasing the right conditions. The best thing you can do to succeed is to choose your territory, despite the current conditions, and positively work it. Do this and you'll be there when the conditions turn to your favor.

> Don't spend your life chasing the right conditions.

Someone once said, "When on the climb you come across a thorn, do not forget that up there, somewhere, is a rose." The man and woman with the stronger spirit keeps looking towards the rose. They know that when they get through to it, they can lead others to it.

There will be times when your spirit languishes and a fever of defeat starts to spread in your camp. I wrote this letter for such a time in my life. It revived a strong spirit in me. There's every possibility these words will help you just the same.

Don't Give Up
(A Letter to the Languishing)

Dear Friend,

If you are here and you are tired of the struggle; if you have seen more pain than gain and you've been working hard for little or no perceivable progress; you've been weary for so long that you've forgotten what it feels like to be rested; it's taking longer than you ever thought it would take and you see those around you seeming to succeed with the success you wish you had. . .

Yes, you are well aware that the road to glory is narrow and yes, you understand that the road is not straight, but of late it's so winding that you wonder if you're not just running around in circles. You've been beaten up, knocked to the ground and kicked, and that's just by your own sense of inadequacy and you just hope that you are able to conceal it with a brave face so that no one notices your discouragement. More than once, you have wondered if it's worth the effort. And you have lost count of how many times you've wanted to give up and drop out.

Well, I have been sent to tell you that if your goal is to not just be a decent father, but to be a great one; if your goal is to be a mother who inspires and teaches her children to do something beautiful with their lives; if your goal is to be a husband who exemplifies the definition of love and courage; to be a wife who by her grace and countenance brings out the best in others; if your goal is to be a parent who sets a tone in the home of peace and security, a parent who leaves a legacy of faith and prosperity for generations to come; if your goal is to be a brother who is dependable, a sister who is trustworthy; if your goal is to be a person who overcomes fears, failures and self criticisms; to be a person who rises above all dis-appointments to make a positive contribution to the lives of others. . .

If your goal is to complete the mission; to stay true to what is right; to be a leader who inspires others to do the same; if your goal is to one day stand before God and hear him say, "Well done good and faithful servant," then by all means, look up, get up, shape up but don't give up. The best things in life happen to those who DON'T GIVE UP!

Sincerely yours,
Wes Beavis

CHAPTER 5

Helping Others Without Getting Frustrated

One of the key steps to the success makeover is to be more intentional in helping others. In a world where needs are many, you would think that helping others is fairly straight forward. But it can be quite the opposite. Whenever people are involved, the complexities increase. Helping people is hard. Helping others is frustrating. That's why so many opt for helping animals and rainforests instead.

My twelve year old son, David, is passionate about the game of basketball. Yesterday, he broke his personal record for spinning a basketball on his finger by keeping it going for twenty-two minutes. Of course I encourage him, but I didn't suggest he learn to do this. It is a skill in which he just decided to become proficient. Something has ignited in his life and he has decided to fan it into flame.

One day, about three years ago, David had watched an NBA game and became so inspired that he asked me if we could go and play on a 'real' basketball court. What he meant was that he wanted to play on a full court, as opposed to the half court in our backyard. So Ellie and I took both of our boys over to the local community park.

> Helping people is hard. That's why so many opt for helping animals and rainforests instead.

Upon arriving at the community park, we discovered that a group of guys were already playing down one end of the basketball court. They were muscular guys and serious about their game. They were playing an intensely physical game and were sweating like race horses at full gallop. I looked at David and saw that he was disappointed. His plans, it seemed, weren't going to work out. In an attempt to bolster his spirit, I told him that all was not lost and that this was a great opportunity for him to watch these capable players and learn from them. I told David to watch how they played the game and to imitate their style. Yes, my son is blessed with a wise father. A father who could put a positive spin on any disappointment. A father who was about to look like a fool.

No sooner had I told David to imitate these guys, when an almighty fight broke out between them. Two of them were on the ground punching and tearing into each other. They were approaching this battle in the same serious and physical way in which they had approached their basketball game. Blood had been drawn and it was getting ugly. My sons were standing there watching all this unfold. 'Oh great,' I thought, with the advice to my sons coming back to haunt me: "Watch these guys and learn from them!" Something had to be done.

Throwing wisdom to the wind, I ran over and threw myself between the two feuding offenders. Somehow, I managed to get them on their feet. With all that was running around my mind in the moment, I wondered how to get their minds off their current activity of wanting to kill each other. A psychological, diversionary tactic might work, so I introduced myself: "Hi guys! My name is Wes. What are your names?"

It seemed to have the right effect. The guy on my right (picture me, wedged between them) told me that his name was Mike. The guy on my left was in the process of telling me that his name was Sam. However, when Sam was distracted, Mike saw his opportunity. He recoiled his fist and sent it towards Sam's face. Sensing some commotion, I looked back towards Mike just in time to collect the fierce blow that he had intended for Sam. Down I went. In front of my family. In front of my sons! One could only imagine what they were learning. Was Dad a peacemaker or an idiot? The only thing certain was that I was on the ground and nothing had been resolved between Mike and Sam. More about this later, I promise!

> Two of them were on the ground punching and tearing into each other.

Success is like eating delicious food. The experience is so good that you want others to enjoy it too claiming, "Hey, this is great. You should try it!" So when the opportunity arises, you encourage people to cook up some success of their own. You are willing to share with them a recipe or two. It's not long before you realize that, while it is a noble desire, you are also making yourself vulnerable to being hurt. What I wanted for Mike and Sam was peace, relational prosperity, and dare I say it, brotherly love! What I got for my noble intent, was a punch in the nose.

One of the early lessons for the successful person is that helping people will hurt you. Now having made such a statement, the obvious question is: If helping people will hurt you, then why bother with helping people? It's a good question and one you will ask every time you are grieved from trying to do something to benefit someone. It's a good question for which you must develop a good answer. Regardless of the pain that it sometimes incurs, let me explain why Ellie and I have opted to help people.

Ellie had just turned twenty when I married her. I was twenty-two. Both of us were on the home stretch in finishing university and college degrees. Neither of us brought any substantial wealth to the marriage table. Over the next fifteen years, we diligently applied the principles of living wisely. We had a vision of becoming completely debt free. We established a plan and stayed committed to the plan until we achieved the goal. The result was that by the time that we were in the afternoon of our thirties, we had the option to retire. Albeit, we would have needed to retire somewhere more fiscally strategic than Beverly Hills. Nonetheless, we could have given up income producing occupations and lived from investment income.

In a sense, we had climbed to the top of a

mountain. The mountain of what to do with our day to day living expenses and how to pay for them had been conquered. We had reached the point of investment-sustaining viability. We had options for how to spend our time. We no longer needed jobs. We could have stayed on the top of that mountain.

Yet, savoring the victory for some time, Ellie and I sensed a new vision emerge. While the thrill of having successfully reached the summit was enjoyable, we came up with this wild idea: Why don't we go back down the mountain and help others climb the mountain too. For we had done it and we knew the way. We decided to become climbing guides for those who wanted to taste victory atop the mountain as well. So in 2001, Ellie and I started Destiny People.

> What I got for my noble intent, was a punch in the nose.

Our vision was simple. We broke it down into what we call the 5 F's: *To help people become successful in their faith, family, friendships, fitness and their finances.* We thought if people could experience victory in these areas, they would surely savor a fuller life. Indeed, what's not to like about that objective? And what's not to like about the tour guides?!

Had we not embarked on the Destiny People journey, we would have missed the greatest growth experience of our lives. Since starting, we have experienced signs of tremendous advancement in the lives of people as we have been climbing the mountain together. Though it has taken us longer than we initially thought to learn to climb as a group, it has been absolutely worth it. And despite the imperfections of the tour guides, the climb has proved to be powerfully beneficial for a lot of people.

Have we been hurt by some people along the way? Absolutely. Are we blaming anyone? No way! In fact, a lot of the times we deserved to be hurt because our thinking was plain dumb. Other times, we have been frustrated because we were naive to the ways some people are wired. The result is that we have hurt ourselves because our expectations of people were way beyond their nature to deliver.

While helping people will sometimes hurt you, the answer is not to abandon your desire to help others. The answer is to understand the dynamics of working with people. To reduce our naiveté increases our ability to help people without getting frazzled with frustration.

Be at Peace With Your Own Imperfections

The first step to helping people is to be reconciled with your own imperfections. If you're not at peace with your own imperfections, you will take issue with everyone else's. The end result is that you become jaded with people and quick to criticize. Sometimes our success can be the very thing that stands in the way of us being a benefit to others. Our tall victories can cause us to

> If you're not at peace with your own imperfections, you will take issue with everyone else's.

develop a short, critical spirit towards those who are not measuring up to their potential.

Many a person blessed with success has sabotaged their positive influence. They simply operate so much out of their success that they become oblivious to their own imperfections and vulnerabilities.

The reality is that the paint isn't quite dry on all of us. We are all a work in progress. Successful people need to recognize this more than those who are struggling. It keeps the sanctimonious pride out and the life-giving compassion in as we seek to help others succeed.

Everyone Chooses Their Own Altitude

Some people fly just high enough not to hit the curb. Why? Because they're comfortable with that altitude. When they look up into the sky, they don't imagine themselves being up there. Dr. David Niven says, "Those who do not expend themselves do so because they cannot see the long-term benefit of work outweighing the short term benefit of laziness." Let's face it, while soaring high brings a lot more reward, it also takes much more effort than flying low. Everyone has the right to fly below their potential if it suits them.

Our role is to help people catch a vision for success. We do so by sharing the joys of living life at a higher altitude. But you cannot argue a person into increase. Marilyn Ferguson, author of *The Aquarian Conspiracy*, says, "No one can persuade another to change. Each of us guards the gate that can only be opened from the inside. We cannot open the gate of another, either by argument or by emotional appeal."

Everyone chooses their own altitude. If you care

> Our role is to help people catch a vision for success. But you cannot argue a person into increase.

about a person's life more than they care about themselves, you are headed for heartache and disappointment. It's okay to want a better life for someone, but keep a degree of detachment to your concern, otherwise people will drive you crazy.

Some Need the Heat

After spending thirty years helping people improve their lives, Dr. Jim Reeve concluded: "People don't change when they see the light, they change when they feel the heat." Take this wisdom with you when you are endeavoring to help someone. Your message might be perfect for them, but they may not be ready. They may not have 'hit bottom' enough yet. Sometimes you'll throw someone a lifeline and they will just let it lay there. Don't exasperate yourself by interpreting their lack of response as a personal rejection. Often, it is just a case of people not being disgusted enough with their plight to be willing to accept the help.

> If you care about a person's life more than they care about themselves, you are headed for heartache and disappointment.

Recently, a man phoned me about the state of

his marriage. He called me at a time in the day and spoke in tones that lead me to the conclusion that his marriage was in desperate trouble. I offered to come and meet with him, to which he replied, "That would be great but can we make it next week. This week is looking really busy for me." He had seen the light but obviously had not felt the heat!

The Baggage Transfer

I learned about 'transference' in my college psychology class. It was when I started helping people that I realized that it wasn't just a theory. Some people have no intention to change, they just want someone to which they can transfer their despairing thoughts and gain a temporary relief. These people set a trap for naive people helpers. Their lives are a mess and they send out an S.O.S. signal indicating that they want to be rescued to a better life. So we, knowing the pathway to a better life, are quick to respond.

We listen, listen and listen some more. But by the time we've heard all their sad stories and are ready to share some valuable insights that would help them, they've switched off. We go ahead and give some advice anyway but something tells us that they have long since checked out. They are not interested in the conversation any more because they have already got what they wanted. They unpacked the mess of their lives to some sympathetic ears and they feel better for having done so. It's only a temporary relief but it's good enough for the moment. They repack their bag of mess and mistakes and move on knowing that when it all gets too much to carry, there will be someone else willing to 'help' them.

Bullfrogs & Butterflies

Let me start with the butterflies first. These are people who don't put down roots anywhere. They are sincerely nice and give you the impression that your brand of help is just what they have been looking for. You're excited because they actually came to you rather than you having to go to them. So you are delighted to spend time with them. But then, you become less than delighted when they move on as quickly as they came leaving you to ask yourself the profound question, "What was that all about?"

You only have to come across a few butterflies to recognize them. They flit around from person to person, from group to group. When you come across a butterfly (or perhaps I should say when they come across you), it's a good time to remind yourself that the proof is in the longevity.

Now for the bullfrogs. They are people that sit

on your lily pad and croak to get your attention. But as soon as you reach out to touch them, they jump off your lily pad onto someone else's. These are the people that think, 'Why would I want to belong to a club that would have me as a member?' It is their low self worth

> I give opportunity to those with promise and potential, but the reward is reserved for those who produce results.

that leads them to yearn for people's attention, especially the attention of successful people.

Bullfrogs think that if they are acknowledged by a successful person, then somehow they will feel better about themselves. But when you eventually acknowledge a bullfrog, their low self value kicks in and convinces them that you must not be that successful if you are willing to be associated with them. So they hop around from person to person, from organization to organization dragging with them their success defeating mentality that 'only losers value losers'.

Mr. & Mrs. Good Potential

Have you ever heard a successful person thank someone else with the words: "You believed in me before I believed in myself?" It's a nice sentiment and I sure appreciate it when it turns out to be the case. But let's be real. If all it took for someone to succeed was to have someone else believe in them, then there would be no failures. The reality is that the world is full of Mr. & Mrs. Good Potentials. After several disappointing experiences of paying people on the basis of their potential, I have revised my strategy. These days I give opportunity to those with promise and potential, but the reward is reserved for those who produce results.

Lovers of Dysfunction

When you have discovered the keys that open the doors to a better life, the obvious audience for your good news is the audience of people who are struggling with issues. So with great enthusiasm, you share with them the principles of success. Then you wait for

> When you help others, your life improves in the process.

them to act upon your freedom bringing revelation. They act not. They remain unchanged.

So you try it again, thinking that you must not have explained it adequately the first time.

Again, they stay engulfed in their issues. Then upon subsequent attempts to help them, you realize that, while they like the attention you are giving them, they actually don't want what you are offering. They are, in fact, in love with their dysfunction. It's their identity. They love the way their dysfunction is their ever present, 'get out of responsibility free' card.

Your first few rounds with these people give you the impression that you are making headway. You believe when all others have failed, your brand of help is going to win the day. Wrong! Far from being the hero, you are about to become their latest casualty. They are a bottomless pit of emotional needs, which no human can fill. They will draw you in with hopeful hyperbole, but at the end of the day, you're being set up. Their intention is to break you over their brokenness. Instead of just being dysfunctional, they want a friend who shares and validates their disorder.

And the worst part of all is that when they discover that you refuse to be broken over their brokenness, they will villainize you. This is not because they dislike you, but in order to maintain their identity as a victim, there has to be a villain. And your reward for trying to help them, is that you get to be the villain! Aren't you just bursting to get out there and help people succeed?

Don't become despondent about helping others. Only one in ten of the people that you try to help will fit into any of the above categories. But you need to know about them because they are the ten percent which will cause ninety percent of your grief in trying to help people. In his book, *Maximize the Moment*, T.D. Jakes provides valuable insight on this matter: "Your efforts to rehabilitate a person may fail. If you are a chronically caped crusader, like I am, you may have this fierce need to help the victim or underdog, but you cannot help everyone. Sometimes you have to accept the fact that your efforts are not enough. Releasing them doesn't mean that the people will never get better. It just means that God is better suited at this than you are. Release them to the One who never fails."

Working with people will always be challenging. The effort will cause you to learn more about people than you care to know. The effort will cause you to learn more about yourself than you care to know! But it is all beneficial when you maintain a positive disposition. While you may fail at helping some, you will be successful at helping others. The bottom line is that when you help others, your life improves in the process.

So what ever happened to Mike and Sam? Well, after being unceremoniously decked, I got back up and reasoned with the one who seemed to be most rational. At that point, it was Sam. I attempted to convince him of the futility of the fight and encouraged him to get in his car and leave. It was a relief to see him act on my advice (without returning with a gun!).

Then I turned to Mike who was still significantly bigger than me and mad as a bull. By that stage, I had nothing to lose. I got in his face and started belting out what could have been the last motivational talk of my life: "Mike, I had just got done telling my sons to watch you guys and learn from you. Then you started fighting like dogs. What am I supposed to tell my sons, Mike? That this is the way that adults solve their differences? C'mon Mike, God put you on the planet to fly like an eagle, not scrap like a dog. You are meant to be an inspiration to kids. They should grow up wanting to be like you. Do you really want to be an example of violence to these kids, Mike?"

My heart was pounding because I had no idea how he was going to respond. I decided to just keep moving forward by asking him a most oblique question, given the tenuous position I was in, "Mike, can I pray for you?" I figured if he was going to kill me, I might as well go out the right way! He nodded.

When I was done, I removed my hand from

Mike's tattooed shoulder. He looked up and I knew that he had been moved. He went over to my sons and apologized to them. Then he headed back over to where his buddies were standing. As Mike got closer to them, they started heralding his success at kicking Sam's butt. But Mike gestured his hands to tell them to stop. He didn't want to revisit the mess from which he had been lifted. So Mike left. He didn't go back. He changed for the better.

The jury is still out as to my wisdom in getting involved in the fight in the first place. Had my sons not been there, perhaps I would not have been so inclined. Nonetheless, it's a good story to tell as an example

> He didn't want to revisit the mess from which he had been lifted.

that helping people opens both the door to the possibility of getting hurt and the door to seeing wonderful changes in people's lives. Most times, you can't have the miracle unless you open yourself to the possibility of getting hurt. But seeing the miracle of transformation in a person's life, makes the risk worthwhile.

CHAPTER 6

Giving up the Excuse and Blame Options

When an archer misses the mark he turns and looks for the fault within himself. Failure to hit the bull's-eye is never the fault of the target. To improve your aim improve yourself.

—Gilbert Arland

It is possible to rise to some level of success and still harbor a propensity to blame and make excuses. I know from experience. But inevitably, there comes a time when any further advancement requires you to remove from your mental repertoire the option to blame and create excuses. Without doubt, it's not an easy thing to do. Blaming someone else or making an excuse that 'gets you off the hook' removes you from being responsible for your conditions. It's not a new propensity. Putting the blame on someone or something else is as old as humanity itself. Though it's not new, I suspect that we have created a societal system that makes it easier than ever before to avoid responsibility.

A perfect example of this happened while a friend named Steve and I were in the food court of a discount mega store. Adjacent to the food court was the 'Returns' department. A few people were waiting in line with merchandise they had purchased but for some reason, they wanted to return for a refund. There was a lady in line who had a cart with two large house plants that were showing no signs of life. In fact, they were so devoid of life that they were not only brown, they were totally crispy. It was obvious that they had been left in the hot California sun for weeks without so much as a drop of water.

> 'It's not my fault' is a thought that keeps too many people delayed on the road of life.

Steve was puzzled. Was this lady, after neglecting her plants to death, going to try and get a refund? Surely the returns clerk was not going to entertain such a notion. But sure enough, without any hesitation, a full refund was awarded. The clerk attached a tag to the plants and wheeled them off to the side. Steve and I wandered over to the cart to read what the clerk had written on the tag. Under the heading 'Reason for Return', the clerk had written in big black letters: Plants Dead.

It seemed preposterous to Steve and me. Why would someone buy two plants, take them home, kill them, then return them to the store to get their money back? It almost seemed illegal. After this, I learned that many stores have a 'no fault' policy to the return of dead plants. The stores have determined that by removing the responsibility for the life of the plants from the customer, it builds goodwill and leads to further sales. Enticements like this are surely reinforcing a growing notion that we have the 'right' not to be responsible.

If you have succeeded to a certain point but sense your progress has slowed down, it's quite likely that you have abdicated responsibility for your advancement. You have established some excuses and surrendered your advancement to them. You prefer to call them legitimate reasons. Whatever you decide to call them, excuses or legitimate reasons, you are making something outside of yourself responsible for your condition. 'It's not my fault' is a thought that keeps too many people delayed on the road of life. Even people at the Bachelor's level of success can be held back from achieving their Master's level of success because they have too much 'it's not my fault' still in them.

"It can't be wrong when it feels so right" is the famous line of a popular song from yesteryear. The thing about making an excuse or placing the blame is that it doesn't even make you feel right. You come away from the exercise feeling like you have just lied to yourself. And the truth is that you should feel 'liar's remorse' because you have just taken a wrecking ball to your future. Here are four reasons why successful people want to eject blame and excuses from their way of managing the circumstances of life.

1) Excuses and blame nourish pessimism.

Every person is free to create their own view of the world. Hammer away at life for long enough and anyone will be given enough material to build a pessimistic view of life. Pessimism is the inclination to expect the worst in any circumstance. No doubt, every successful person sees a lot of hard realities and unfairness in their journey. Despite their successes, some still allow the difficulties of life to negatively form their world view. This doesn't negate their achievements, but it makes you wonder how much more impacting they could be if they were guided by an optimistic nature.

Blame and excuse are roommates with

pessimism. They live together. They help each other out. They feed and support one another. Blame and excuse moved in with pessimism when they were evicted from the house of optimism.

More good things flow to people who expect good outcomes than flow to those who expect poor outcomes. When blame and excuse walk down the street, the optimist will cross to the other side because better stuff happens in the absence of these dubious fellows.

2) Excuses and blame grow a victim mentality.

Sometimes, it is easier to blame your parents, your education, your genes, or your bad luck for your current circumstances. Yet, each time you choose to make an excuse or blame something or someone for your circumstances, you abdicate your responsibility for advancement. You allow yourself to become the victim. Acquiring a victim mentality doesn't happen overnight.

> More good things flow to people who expect good outcomes than flow to those who expect poor outcomes.

A victim mentality is grown. It blooms in the soil of destructive thinking. Soil that is well fertilized with a bag of blame and an endless supply of excuses.

It doesn't matter how successful you are, your next advancement might provide the perfect conditions for you to start growing a victim mentality. You will know that you are fostering these conditions if you start to reach

> To avoid looking like a goose, we lay down an excuse.

for the 'bag-o-blame'. Resist having the mindset of a victim. Instead, consider the words of American novelist and journalist, Joan Didion: "The willingness to accept responsibility for one's own life is the source from which self-respect springs."

3) Excuses and blame breed defeat and despair.

No one ever feels a sense of victory as a result of making an excuse. It may bring temporary relief but it is short lived. Like cheap paint on a wall, it can't cover what lies beneath and what lies there is the fact that we've been whooped by something. It hurts to admit it so we try a quick fix with the words: "It's not my fault." But the quick fix never works the way we want. Instead of saving face, excuses cause us to face deeper feelings of defeat and despair.

Making excuses and placing the blame are self-defense mechanisms. They are ways that help us to preserve our dignity when the circumstances of life shine a spotlight on the limits of our competency. Rather than admit that we have limitations, we move the spotlight off ourselves to highlight something else.

Nobody likes having their incompetence revealed. It is humiliating to have the spotlight revealing our intellectual nakedness. Making an excuse or placing some blame is a natural thing to do when we hit the ceiling of our competency. However, taking that course of action does nothing to raise the ceiling. When you blame others, you give up your power to learn, change, increase your competency and advance your life.

4) Excuses and blame delay victory.

Let's face it, how we are perceived by others is important to us. If we were birds, we would much rather be an eagle than a goose. So it's understandable that when life exposes our incompetence, to avoid looking like a goose, we lay down an excuse. It's quick, convenient and if we lay it just right, it can make us look downright commanding.

However, for as long as we have an excuse or someone to blame, we avoid taking responsibility for our own advancement. Rationalizations and justifications do nothing but delay victory. As Dr.

Phillip McGraw states: "While you are passion-ately blaming someone else, your self-diagnostic skills simply fall apart." The end result is that we have stunted our growth and our future victory is delayed.

No one wants to stop their life from increasing in value, yet that's what happens when we make excuses. If we accommodate our excuses, our life will be governed by our excuses. If we accommodate the practice of blaming someone or something else for our current position in life, we will neglect the practice of evalu-ating our position and providing the best conditions for our advancement. Why then, knowing the dismal consequences, do we make such accommodations?

> To completely eradicate 'blame placing' and 'excuse fabricating' from your life is a key to your advancement.

To completely eradicate 'blame placing' and 'excuse fabricating' from your life is a key to your advancement. It is an essential component of the success makeover.

CHAPTER 7

Fear Protection for the Successful Person

I s it possible to be so successful that you no longer have fear? I have spoken with multi-millionaires and listened to them express enormous concerns over their wealth. I have met men who have married the woman of their dreams only to spend their days worrying about the possibility of losing her to another man. I have met women with everything going for them, privately anxious about their husband remaining committed to 'forsaking all others'. There are perfectly healthy people who fear that they are targets for a disease that 'runs in the family'; high positioned leaders who can't relax their grip on the leadership reins for fear of losing their position, and people endowed with popularity who go to great measures to shield their kids from being recognized.

Far from reducing your fears, success makes you more susceptible to fear. With every increase in your personal life, so do your opportunities for anxiety increase. It comes down to this truth: As you work to make your life large, fear will be working to make your life small. I recently experienced a perfect example of this truth.

> As you work to make your life large, fear will be working to make your life small.

Whilst staying at our home in the mountains, I went for a morning run to start the day. Alongside a bend in the road was a red house. As I ran past it, a very robust Rottweiler dog who was ferociously offended by my presence came bounding out of the house. Fortunately, the owner was able to call the dog back before it added a bite to its intimidating bark. As I needed to run past this same house on my way back, I politely urged the owner to keep his dog restrained. He gave a compliant nod.

Rounding out my run, I was again running past the red house on the bend. To my amazement, the dog came at me for a second time. After calling out, the owner reappeared to retrieve his dog.

This time, I was more earnest in my request. In light of the fact that my kids walk this same road on the way to the lake, I implored him to keep his dog restrained. He agreed and promised to keep him leashed.

The next morning as I was preparing to enjoy another run, I contemplated heading in a different direction. But then I thought that would be giving into my fears. Others may be governed by their fears, but not Wes Beavis! So, off I ran boldly in the direction of the red house. Admittedly, I was a little nervous but I was determined not to be afraid. As I rounded the

> He landed with his canine teeth firmly anchored in my calf muscle.

bend, I passed the red house just in time to see 'it' in my peripheral vision.

Like he had just jumped out of a Stephen King movie, the dog came after me. He was ten feet away when he leapt into the air with a 'visual lock' on my right leg. His saliva slobbered lips retracted and he landed with his canine teeth firmly anchored in my calf muscle.

This time, I was not polite. Screaming for the owner, I reached for my cell phone and called the emergency hotline. The police arrived and charged the owner with a felony misdemeanor, confiscated his dog for a ten day quarantine, issued him with a fine and a court date. As for me, after the medical treatment of a tetanus shot and a course of antibiotics, I healed to run again. Albeit with a some scars on my leg and a few in my mind.

For the first few times after the 'Rottweiler Incident', it was nauseating to run past the red house. One time, the anxiety was so overwhelming that I almost vomited. There was the option to stop running in the mountains. But to respond that way meant that my fear of that dog would have made my world small. I worked to keep my world large. I have not completely elimi-

> Be motivated by something which develops and enlarges your world, not contracts it.

nated my wariness of vicious mutts. But armed with a protective tennis racquet, I am still running much to the intrigue of fellow mountain dwellers who ask, "Where is the tennis court?"

It is naive to think that success will eliminate your fears. If you are neurotic about money when your net worth is one hundred dollars, to increase your net worth to a million dollars will not deliver you from your neurosis but in fact increase it. As you advance, you must be mindful that fear is an ever present challenge. You never entirely eliminate fear because with every advancement, you become aware of new issues that can strangle the peace out of you. As the saying goes, "There's a devil at every level." Watch the people who advance. They press on. Not because fear is absent, but because they include the presence of a few protective tennis racquets!

Tennis Racquet #1:

Avoid Being Motivated by Fear

Remind yourself that while fear is a motivator, it's not a good one. Certainly, fear can propel you into action. For example, a fear of detention may motivate a child to complete his or her homework. But it's an inferior motivator. Fear drains optimism

> Nobody's life is a chain of unbroken victories.

and passion. Fear depletes confidence and dries up enthusiasm. As it limits your world, opportunities and beneficial relationships will be missed.

Sure fear can bolster you forward, but it will transform you in the process. The late Larry Burkett illustrates an example of the transformation process: "Many decisions people make are motivated by fear of the future. For example, people scrimp and sacrifice for the elusive day known as retirement. Often the total focus of the earlier years is toward the eventual day when 'we can relax and enjoy ourselves'. Unfortunately, the same fear that prompted hoarding for the 'latter' years leads to further sacrifices 'just in case'."

Being motivated by fear turns you into a far cry from what you could have become, had you been motivated by something more positive. Motivation that is based upon something positive, such as a desire to advance in the direction of your vision, will expand you.

> Doubt and fear look at what you're going through, but faith looks at where you are going to. So build your faith.

Be motivated by something which develops and enlarges your world, not contracts it.

Tennis Racquet #2:

Focus on Improvement Rather Than What You Fear

Do you fully understand what happens when you fear something? Rather than defending yourself against it, worrying actually gives fear a 'foot in the door' of your life. Be assured it's just a matter of time until fear moves in and takes complete control. The successful business man known in the Bible as Job testified to it when he wrote: "What I feared has come upon me; what I dreaded has happened to me."

There's only so much available space in that precious life of yours. Why dedicate some of that limited space to something that drags you down? It's best to give the space in your life to that which will elevate your position. Spending time worrying about what we fear and what may go wrong takes precious time away from improving and elevating the quality of your life. In other words, worrying about things going wrong increases the chances that they will go wrong.

Tennis Racquet #3:

Define Failure as an Event Not an Identity

Ask anyone who has lived a long life whether they have any regrets and most will focus on the things they didn't do rather than what they did do. They lament the things they failed to try rather than the things they tried and failed. The reality is that we fear failing so much that we play it safe. Rather than living to our big and large potential, our lives end up being smaller because of fear.

The movie, *The Legend of Baggar Vance*, is about a professional golfer named Rannulph Junuh, played by Matt Damon. Rannulph Junuh loses his golf swing which is apparently the nightmare of every golfer. In from nowhere walks caddy Baggar Vance, played by Will Smith, who helps him to get his swing back. My favorite line of the movie is when Rannulph is in the middle of a major golf tournament. He slices the ball badly and murmurs to his caddy Baggar Vance, "This is going to be embarrassing." To which Baggar Vance replies, "No, it's been embarrassing for some time now!"

So many people resist taking a shot at the next level for fear of embarrassing themselves if they fail. So they hold back in the name of self-preservation, not realizing that every time they do, they are making their world smaller. Nobody's life is a chain of unbroken victories. Define failure according to what it is, an event. It's never an identity unless you allow it to be. In the words of Marilyn vos Savant: "Being defeated is only a temporary condition; giving up is what makes it permanent."

Tennis Racquet #4:

Conquer Fear with Faith

As an emerging leader, you must realize that

your fears will impact more than just yourself. As psychologist Daniel Goleman says, "Leaders who can't master their own fears can thus infect an entire group." You will go through uncertain times, but as a good leader, you don't pass a spirit of anxiety on to your team. That doesn't mean you deny the existence of danger (the Rottweiler doesn't exist, the Rottweiler doesn't exist), as this doesn't reassure your team. Remind yourself that doubt and fear look at what you're going through, but faith looks at where you are going to. So build your faith. Because armed with your tennis racquet of faith, you can run right through uncertain territory taking many people with you.

Keep working to make your life large. As you do, realize that your fears will be working just as hard to make your life small. With absolute certainty, if you stop taking risks then you get intimidated. And intimidation does not give birth to success. To remind myself of this, I wrote myself a poem called Ode to The Foe, which I hereby share with you.

Ode To The Foe

Every victor is only so because there was a foe
But if a foe I never know because I'm scared to go
Then never will I victory see
Or victory have to show

Wes Beavis

CHAPTER 8

Your Friends are the Bridges to Your Future

Greek philosopher, Euripides (c.480-406 B.C.), said, "It's a good thing to be rich and a good thing to be strong, but it is a better thing to be loved by many friends." Australian philosopher, Wes Beavis (1962- A.D.), says, "It's good to be loved by many friends, and even better when some of them are rich and strong."

More than our circumstances, the people with whom we connect can change our lives. The quality of our tomorrow is largely influenced by those with whom we congregate today. If you want to advance in life, check your relationships. Your progression depends on them. Your friends are the bridges to your future.

When you think about the times in your life

when you have experienced dramatic change, there were people involved. The quality of the change often reflects the quality of the people you associated with at the time.

Philip Baker leads an organization of four thousand people in Perth, Australia, the most geographically remote city in the world. Though vastly separated in distance, he has been purposeful in building relationships with great leaders around the world. Several very successful leaders in America travel the arduous twenty hour flight to Perth, so they can take part in what Philip is doing. A lot of Philip's success is attributed to him living this principle: "Our destiny is not so much in us. It's in other people. So as we build relationships, we are building bridges to our future."

> "As we build relationships, we are building bridges to our future."

Seek Relationships that Enlarge You

Euripides was right to say that a man with many friends is blessed. However, this kind of bridge building takes more than having lots of friends. Otherwise, you could pony up to the bar in any one of a million pubs in the world and build yourself an army of friends. If building bridges to a better future is your goal, you need to have some relationships with people who are already living that better future. Moving forward requires you to discern the difference between the people who lessen you and the people who enlarge you.

Recently, I was on the tail end of a phone conversation when my son, David, came into my office. When I hung up the phone, he asked me who I was talking to. I told him that I was talking to Maya from our insurance company. David thought for a moment and then asked, "Dad, was she making your life easier or harder?" I was taken with my son's question. It was insightful for a twelve year old. The more I thought about it,

> Have some relationships with people who are already living that better future.

the more I realized that I should be asking that question a lot more with regard to my relationships. Sometimes, people slip into our lives who make life harder, with no mind for our benefit.

Take careful note of what business expert, Peter Drucker, says, "It makes no sense to settle for relationships that lessen rather than enlarge us, that diminish rather than develop our values and character. Thus, we should summon the courage and integrity to abandon dead-end personal or work relationships. We need to recognize how murky notions of loyalty can blind us to simple realities and how unrealistic hopes that things will change can prevent us from achieving our higher potential. Toxic relationships not only make us unhappy; they corrupt our attitudes and dispositions in ways that undermine healthier relationships and blur our vision of what is possible. It's never easy to change, but nothing gets better without change."

Advancing in life requires you to make changes in your relational life. Part of this change is to let some relationships burn out. Rarely do you need to take a fire extinguisher to a relationship. A relationship is like a campfire. If

> Many try to keep every relationship alive and end up feeling overwhelmed and guilty about not doing a good job with any relationship.

you don't add fuel to it, given enough time, it will naturally burn out.

While a relationship will burn out if it is starved

of fuel, sometimes you have to make a conscious decision to stop fueling it. Even if a relationship has dwindled down to being on life support with only an occasional phone call, there is always a reticence to admit that it's over. If there is any milk of human kindness running in your veins, deciding that a friendship has no future seems judgmental, cruel, and makes you feel like you are being elitist. For this reason, many try to keep every relationship alive and end up feeling overwhelmed and guilty about not doing a good job with any relationship. It's okay to release a relationship that has had its day

> In order to progress, you need to make new friends.

and run its course. Get out of their lives so they, too, can have room for someone new!

Then there are those relationships that won't die out naturally. The other party is needy and emotional. In this case, I defer to some old fashioned advice: "If your head is in the jaws of a lion, wriggle out nice and slow." In other words, end it gradually but do end it.

This is not to say you can't maintain some relationships for 'old times sake' and other senti-mentalities. In fact, I am wary of people who don't have some long term friendships. When people only have 'recent' friends and no old friends, it is usually an indication that they are bereft of what it takes to sustain relationships over the long haul. By all means have some old friends, but know that in order to progress, you need to make new friends.

Put People in Your Life Who Broaden You

We are prone to getting stuck in ruts. It's a byproduct of discovering something that works and we stick with it for that reason. Psychologists refer to this behavior as set neural pathways or habituation. It is important to the flow of our lives to

> The best way to launch yourself into the next level is to connect with someone who is already living at the next level.

have some components which run on automated pilot. It means we don't have to evaluate our every motion and thought during the day. Once some thoughts and actions are tested with pleasing results, we incorporate those thoughts and actions into our daily routine. There is no need to keep testing them.

When we want to improve our life, however, it

means we have to build new thoughts and actions into our routine so that we can get new results. For many people, the dreams of a new or improved life come unstuck because, whilst they dream of new results, they stick with their normal routine of thoughts and actions.

> **If you build the bridge, getting the opportunity to cross it will be inevitable. The best relationships take years to build but they last even longer.**

The same happens when we try to advance whilst keeping the same line up of relationships.

Relationships are so key to our advancement that unless we make changes to our line up of relationships, we are going to remain exactly where we are—stuck in the rut of our current success. The best way to launch yourself into the next level is to connect with someone who is already living at the next level. They are at that level because they are doing things different from you. Seeing what they are doing differently will challenge you to climb out of the rut that has led you this high, but can't lead you any higher.

Sometimes a new relationship will open doors

of opportunity for you. WARNING: Do not allow this to be your motivation. The primary focus of connecting with someone more successful than you should be to gain from their wisdom and inspiration, not to get them to give you a break. Nothing will sabotage the budding friendship quicker than if they smell opportunism.

If you respectfully build a genuine association, then over time new opportunities will naturally flow. If you build the bridge, getting the opportunity to cross it will be inevitable. Be patient. Focus on building a strong bridge. The best relationships take years to build but they last even longer.

> Everyone needs new associations regardless of their level.

Make Room for New Associations

To make room for new associations, some older associations may need to be released. Some might feel that adding and eliminating associations for the purpose of improving one's life is being utilitarian; viewing people for what you can get out of them. That is not the best spirit by which to view this principle. Consider it from the opposite side.

When a person succeeds, something is liberated within them that makes them want to help others succeed. Albeit they have to distinguish between those who genuinely want help, and those who simply want to sun bathe in the aura of someone successful. But in the scheme of life, everyone needs new associations regardless of their level. The proverb, "As iron sharpens iron, so one man sharpens another," establishes that every new association has the potential to sharpen both parties.

Sometimes it's hard to tell whether a current association has run its course or whether it's just hibernating, waiting for a more suitable season. Here's one way to determine the future value of a relationship. Look at your friend's friends. Because your friend is on his way to becoming like his friends. If you like what you see, stay connected. But if

> It is not right for people of promising potential to miss out on your input because someone else is depleting your energy and replacing it with turmoil.

you are not inspired by what you see, it's time to bid the relationship farewell. Don't see it as abandoning them. As I said before, removing yourself from their life creates room for them to have new associations.

Release Friends that Don't Value Your Improvements

If you have a bucket of crabs and one crab decides to climb out of the bucket, the other crabs will reach up and pull it back down into the bucket. The same can happen to people. Not everyone grows at the same rate. In that personal growth demands the forfeiting of comfort, some stop growing altogether leaving others to grow right past them. When this happens between friends, it introduces a disparage that, most always, can never be reconciled.

As you improve, some of your friends will not recognize your improvements. They will relate to you as you were, not as you are now. It is a hard leap for them to accept the new you. For to recognize your advancements means that they are confronted with their own lack of advancement. To acknowledge your growth, they have to accept that the life that you once shared no longer exists. The dynamics have forever changed. It's just plain easier for them to try to drag you back to your previous level.

T.D. Jakes sums it up this way, "It is sad to realize, but often people who knew you way back when do not have the ability to know you now. They generally assess your potential based on their perspective of your past. They keep you stuck in a stage of your life that is past and gone. These people define you on the basis of who you were, not what you have become, and certainly not who you can someday be." That is why it's hard for a prophet to get honor in his home town. People find it difficult to see the 'new you' because they are looking through glasses that are tinted with the memory of the 'old you'.

If you feel somebody tugging you back into your old bucket, be kind to them. They probably don't realize they're doing it. They just want to keep life with the 'old you' alive. But you know you could never return to that bucket and be happy. There's always the possibility that you can inspire them to climb out of the bucket themselves! You will soon know if that's the case. And if it's not, graciously move on.

End Draining Associations

Keep in mind that while there are people that you admire, there are people who admire you. It is inevitable given your current success. Some people are yet to achieve what you have achieved. They would benefit from your input in their lives. It is not right for people of promising potential to miss out on your input because someone else is depleting your energy and replacing it with turmoil.

Associations that drain the life out of you need to be ended. In her poem *Two Kinds of People*, Ella Wheeler-Wilcox describes these associations as "people who lean". The one who always leans will sap your energy and dampen your enthusiasm. For the sake of your sanity, but more so, for the sake of those who will be better stewards of your input, release those who lean. Make room for "people who lift".

Two Kinds of People

There are two kinds of people on the earth today
Just two kinds of people, no more, I say
Not the good and the bad, for it is well understood
That the good are half bad and the bad are half good
Not the rich and the poor, for to rate a man's wealth
You must first know the state of his conscience and health
Not the happy and sad, for the swift flying years
Bring each man his laughter and each man his tears
No the two kinds of people on earth I mean
Are the people who lift and the people who lean

Ella Wheeler-Wilcox

Every man and woman is endowed with all that it takes to be a 'lifter'. Along the pathway in your journey forward, there are up and coming lifters seeking your inspiration. Giving them the benefit of your friendship and association helps them build bridges to their destiny.

CHAPTER 9

Presenting an Authentic Successful Posture

One of the most spectacular business failures that the business world has ever seen was Texas based, energy giant, Enron Incorporated. The losses were unprecedented. Not only were there millions of stockholders left holding a bag full of nothing, but the retirement savings of all the employees were completely vested in the company. One morning, they awoke to the news that their jobs no longer existed and worse, that all their savings for retirement were wiped out. Chuck Colson wrote of the company, "Enron was no sleazy, backroom bucket shop. It involved the best and brightest pillars of the community. Enron chairman Kenneth Lay boasted that he hired only graduates of the top business schools—Harvard and Wharton."

Before the collapse, Enron exhibited all the features of success. Only those who were privy to the company's 'creative accounting' practices knew that the company was, in reality, a house of cards. When in the global marketplace there was a change in the economic climate, which inevitably happens, Enron was unable to withstand the blow of an ill-wind. Today, Enron is the poster child for corporate scandal and deceit.

> When people scratch below the surface of your success, you want them to find more than just more surface.

You have to ask the question: "How could something that had the elite look of success emerge as a failure of criminal proportions?" It's easy when you live in a world where 'perception is reality'. You make yourself look more successful than you really are and you trade on that perception. That's exactly what Enron did. They traded on the impression of success. Their posture looked successful but it was far from authentic.

If you are going to be successful at being successful, you must learn how to authentically present yourself as such. When people scratch below the surface of your success, you want them to find more than just more surface. You want them to discover substance and strength. Warren Buffett says, "He who swims without shorts in the shallows, swims naked when the tide goes out."

The tide went out on the fifty-five year old man who lived in our street. Shortly after I moved my family into our home, I was informed that this neighbor was the street's premier millionaire. I was duly impressed. He was reputed to have a thriving business. He drove the latest red Corvette which he parked on the black and white checkered, tiled floor of his garage. He had two Harley Davidson's and the front yard to his opulent home was filled with fully grown palm trees. The reason why he paid the exorbitant price for fully matured palm trees was because he didn't want to wait ten years for immature trees to grow. In a sense, he was right. He didn't have ten years to wait. Later that year, he went into battle against a heart attack and lost. The tide went out and with it, the reputation of his ultra-millionaire status. He was found naked on most accounts.

> **We are a combination of better stuff and lesser stuff.**

Speaking to his former wife in the weeks that followed, I realized how his success posture had not been authentic. She had relinquished the title to being his wife years ago. When I asked her how things were going with settling his affairs, she told me it was a nightmare. His business was worthless and was being propped up with credit card debt. Any equity in the home had long been sucked out and spent. She told me that he had bought the two Harley Davidson's to entice his son to spend time with him. A strategy that never worked. Weeks later, the bank foreclosed on the home which was several months delinquent in mortgage payments. When all was said and done, it was going to be a struggle to pay for the funeral.

Perception may be reality, but for a limited time only. While there is some merit in the concept of 'fake it until you make it', eventually there must be bone-fide strength and substance that underlies a person's success.

> What we say either increases our value or cheapens us.

This is the only foundation that will stand the inevitable changing tides. Without such a foundation, we're likely to end up being another Enron in the ocean of life. We'll be standing in the nude when the tide goes out because of a change in conditions. Not an endearing sight for our friends and certainly, a chilling experience for us.

Do you want your success to be genuine and lasting? Establish a posture of success that not only looks inspiring but when people scratch beneath the surface, they discover strength and substance. Anyone can swim boldly when the tide is in their favor. This chapter is about swimming boldly regardless of what the tide is doing. Here are the hallmarks of presenting an authentically successful posture.

1) Operate from the top of your barrel.

We are all a barrel of stuff. Our collection of good motives and experiences are mixed with lesser motives and experiences. We are a combination of better stuff and lesser stuff. A barrel of cream and rocks. The cream, our better self, rises to the top. The rocks, our lesser self, settle to the bottom. The person who exhibits a posture of authentic success learns to operate from the top of their barrel not the bottom.

You can have a degree of success but still spend a lot of time operating out of the bottom of your barrel. If you are motivated by your insecurities, your pride, your anger, your wanting to 'get revenge', your craving to be approved by others, then you are operating out of the bottom of your barrel. Making excuses, placing blame, being judgmental, being consumed with self and fear, are all products of operating from the bottom of your barrel. These things reflect the fact that you are operating out of your lesser self.

If you want to advance to greater levels of success, you need to discipline, change, and elevate yourself to operate from the top of your barrel. Be committed to your better self by operating from the place where pride, insecurity and other non-productive inclinations have been banished.

2) Make your talk profit you not cheapen you.

When law enforcement officers arrest someone, they are mandated to inform that person of their Miranda rights. The first right is 'the right to remain silent'. Why? Because the propensity of human nature is to gabble ourselves downwards. After years of listening to people, I have come to this conclusion: The more we talk, the greater the potential is that we will incriminate ourselves by what we say.

There's a proverb that says, "The tongue has the power of life and death." In other words, what we say can either add life or subtract life. What we say either increases our value or cheapens us. What we say either creates opportunity or closes the door to opportunity. So for goodness sake, talk in a way that advantages you as you face your future.

When facing a challenge, 'talk the answer' rather than 'talking the problem'. Experience has taught me that talking the problem gives life to the problem. It keeps it alive and pre-eminently positioned in your mind.

There is some cathartic relief in sharing your dilemma but be careful with whom you share it. If you share it with the wrong person, you are going to be perceived as a whiner and complainer. If you talk about your challenges with someone who has not gone through them themselves, their lack of sensitivity will further your frustration.

> "If you care about your feelings, talk about your problems; but if you care about your future, don't talk about them."
>
> Gregory Dickow

If you share it with someone who hasn't got the resources or inclination to help, you are setting yourself up for a dive to the bottom of your barrel. Gregory Dickow, host of the *Changing Your Life* program, wisely sums it up: "If you care about your feelings, talk about your problems; but if you care about your future, don't talk about them."

I'm not telling you to deny the presence of problems in your life. That would be living in denial which is mentally unhealthy and will lead to breakdown further along the journey. Everyone has mountains which they are trying to conquer. The difference that separates the strong from the weak is in how we address them. If you talk ABOUT your mountains, you magnify them. If you talk AT your mountains, you can reduce them (providing you say the right things!).

> Successful people need never to travel the low road on anything.

People with an authentic success posture spend more time talking at their mountains than talking to others about their mountains.

Don't let your words cheapen you. When you say to someone, "Let's get together," but you never act on your words, that is cheap talk. It degrades you. Better that you don't say anything than say words that sets you up to look cheap.

The improvements required by your success makeover means that you must eliminate using socially marginal vocabulary (swearing, cussing, and cursing). While dropping the occasional rough word may add some color and impact, it is the low road of communication. Successful people need never to travel the low road on anything.

A few years ago, I was a guest speaker at a major business event. I was excited because one of the other speakers was well renowned. I had read his books and admired his presentations on the Oprah show. So, to have the opportunity to spend some time talking with him backstage, was a dream come true. As we spoke, he included a vast selection of profanities in his discourse. It was sad to hear him cheapen himself with every rogue word. Maybe some would have appreciated him more for the way he spoke. I couldn't help but appreciate him less. Coarse language will hurt your posture more than it will help it.

3) Get in the press until the oil flows.

It takes a lot more to talk positively than just talking positively. To fluently speak the language of success, it has to originate from the core of your human experience. Otherwise, you are just picking up a bullhorn and flapping positive hype. The most powerful success talk is formed deep within your spirit and wells up from there. It comes from getting into the press of life and staying there until your oil flows. Let me explain what I mean.

Have you ever heard a speaker that has that

special something? It's hard to define but you surely know the difference when one speaker has it and the other one doesn't. It is a special quality that enables them to speak with confidence and authority. They are not trying to make a good impression. They don't need to for their 'special sauce' is making it for them.

Jentzen Franklin, a great communicator himself, said that when he was starting out as a speaker he would look at someone with the 'special sauce all over them' and wonder how they got it. He would ask himself: How did they become like that? What books did they read? What schools did they attend? It wasn't until he sensed the anointing of the special sauce appearing on himself that Jentzen knew the answer. It doesn't come from reading books or going to a particular seminar or school; it comes from climbing into the vice of life and getting squeezed until the oil starts flowing.

The special sauce comes out of you when you stay the course of being squeezed by difficulties, heartbreaks and realizing your own incompetence. When you stay committed, even when every fiber of your body wants relief and wants out; when you go through the refiner's fire and pass through the raging waters but keep moving forward rather than opting out, that's when you are anointed with the special sauce.

People, like olives, will only deliver their oil when pressed. You can drive an expensive car, have a beautiful big house with fashionable furniture, wear elite jewelry with the finest clothes, but if you keep jumping out of the vice whenever it gets tough, you will always lack the oil of authentic success.

Many people look good but scratch beneath the surface and you will uncover an unformed, unsuccessful, inclination to quitting, spirit. Yes, we live in a world whereby we can Enron our way around town for a while. But come some challenging conditions, we will be upstaged by a human olive every time! Do you want

> **People, like olives, will only deliver their oil when pressed.**

the posture of someone authentically successful? Then, get in the press and stay there until your oil starts to flow.

4) Be upbeat.

Recently, I was speaking at a conference with Rudy Ruettiger. He spoke of playing football for Notre Dame and then convincing Tri-Star Pictures to make a movie of his life. On the basis of his experiences, Rudy concluded that we take ourselves too seriously and people too personally. His challenge: Be upbeat! By virtue of the magnitude of his accomplishments, I take what he says seriously!

By nature, we beat up ourselves and let life do the same to us, leaving us anything but upbeat. If you want to wear the image of authentic success, you must take corrective measures to banish your insecurities, the orientation towards self, and the fear of what other people think of you. These things produce a downbeat persona and erode your success posture. You may not even realize it, but other people do, and that's why you keep getting passed over when the opportunities are handed out.

> If what makes you lean towards downcast timidity can be fixed, then fix it. If it can't be fixed, then get over it.

If what makes you lean towards downcast timidity can be fixed, then fix it. If it can't be fixed, then get over it. But don't let the world miss out on your upbeat self. And don't miss out on a world of opportunities because you drag your dour self around.

Set the switch of your disposition to enthusiasm

and weld it permanently in that position. Some people get the message about being upbeat but they have trouble with consistency. Being upbeat fifty percent of the time is no better than being dour on a fulltime basis. Success makes you a potential leader. But when your enthusiasm is seasonal, you make it impossible for people to follow you. They can't track with the roller coaster characteristics of your manner.

> When your enthusiasm is seasonal, you make it impossible for people to follow you. They can't track with the roller coaster characteristics of your manner.

Discipline yourself to be consistently upbeat—in season, out of season, and in-between seasons. Chisel into the granite of your mind the saying: "Power does not flow to the dour." If you want substance and strength to be the hallmarks of your success posture, then get yourself a good, consistent, upbeat spirit.

5) Do it to improve not to impress.

Who of us has not endeavored to achieve something noteworthy to impress someone?

Tremendous victories are often gained in the hope that it will win the favor and approval of others. While it may be better than not being motivated at all, it's not the greatest motivation.

There are problems with improving your life in the hope that you will gain (or regain) someone's affection. First, you set yourself up to have your victory tinged with disappointment if those you're seeking to impress look at your results with ambivalence. Second, and more significant, being motivated by a hunger for approval means that you will always be restless. If you're not enough without it, you'll never be enough with it. There will always be the need to be validated by just one more person, association, or organization.

> **Being motivated by a hunger for approval means that you will always be restless.**

Bottom line, accept who you are. Then, seek to improve yourself. Ironically, the net result of doing this is that some people will be impressed. This is better seen as an added bonus rather than a basic necessity.

6) Be free of personal debt.

I deal with this subject extensively in my book, *Escape to Prosperity*. There is nothing quite like living your life without personal debt. To own your home, vehicles and all other fun goods and chattels will bring strength and substance to your success posture. When you make the last payment on your home mortgage, you'll discover just what I mean. You walk a little taller with more certainty through the maze of life as a result of not being beholden to a lender.

7) Create your own success trends.

I heard it said recently that the key to happiness is to get more or be content with less. The truth of this we can't ignore. When you clear the smoke, the goal of most advertising is to release a spirit of discontent within you for what you have. How else are they going to get you to buy their product if they don't first convince you that you can't be happy unless you have their product?

I am not going to 'get down' on getting more. Neither am I going to validate being content with less, if it becomes an excuse for you not advancing boldly in the direction of your potential. What I am advocating is that you must set your own definition of success rather than having the commercial marketplace set it for you. Here's why.

Let's say that you had the resources to buy the latest recommendation of everything. In every department of life from diamond rings to kitchen things, from clothes to cars, from homes to yards, from planes to boats, from gadgets to goats, you get the very best of everything. Once you have finalized your purchases, how long will the marketplace leave you alone? As long as it takes for them to design something better, which by today's technological pace, is not very long.

Those who walk with an authentic success posture don't profane of 'getting better things', they just refuse to allow the market to bully them into thinking that they are less without them. They establish their own success trends in accordance with their personal advancement goals. They resist being driven by success trends, but rather they pick and choose, in line with their principles for living.

8) Move into your optimum weight zone.

In this section, I am writing for those who are in excess of their optimum weight. For those beanstalks who don't battle with this, you can skip your svelte selves right down to the next section!

Admittedly, this is where the playing field of

life is uneven. Some people can consume all they want, of what they want, whenever they want, and not gain an ounce. Others walk past a bakery and put on weight just smelling the aroma. This predicament is not helped by the fact that our metabolism slows as we mature. It is ironic that when our budgets can handle rich foods,

> It is ironic that when our budgets can handle rich foods, our bodies can't.

our bodies can't. And with every increase to our clothing size, we experience a decrease to our success posture.

It is easier to talk like a success, dress like a success and stride like a success when you are in your optimum weight zone. I can testify to this from personal experience. I never considered myself to be significantly overweight. I thought I was just carrying a few extra pounds. My doctor saw it differently. He calculated my excesses to be initiating a major assault on my internal organs. My literal future was in jeopardy. For the first time in my life, I took seriously how much I should weigh according to given my height. It took six months to recalibrate to my optimum weight—a size I hadn't been in fifteen years. It has been the single most elevating factor in my personal success makeover.

9) Be punctual.

You know how it feels when you arrive to an appointment on time as opposed to how you feel when you arrive late. The difference of just minutes either side of the appointment time changes everything as to how you carry yourself. It's hard to maintain the upright walk in your success spirit when the first words you utter to your appointee are, "Sorry I'm late."

10) Be time wealthy.

We live in an age when being busy is worn as a badge of honor. To say to someone, "I know that you're very busy" is another way of saying, "You are more successful than me and I honor you." Busyness has become such an acceptable way of life that thoughtlessness and bad manners is somehow excused because 'we are busy'.

Living a harried life of constantly being busy is not a success symbol. It is an indication that you are guilty of life mismanagement. If you want an authentic success posture, be time wealthy. Be savvy enough in your leadership of life to create margins when you are, contrary to modern culture, un-busy. It's the new success symbol. Wear it with pride. Who knows, you may re-discover the lost art of contemplation and reflection which are both powerful influences in personal development.

11) Take out an Integrity Policy.

From time to time, I hear speakers espouse the virtues of integrity being essential to gaining success. But let me tell you the way it is. Integrity alone will not cause you to be a success. Too many other ingredients are required. But integrity alone does ensure that you will maintain your success. Enron Incorporated had a slew of Harvard and Wharton degrees hanging on its walls. But for lack of integrity, those walls were destroyed.

> "It's not how high you jump, it's how straight you walk when you hit the ground. That's the bottom line of success."
>
> Dr. Jim Reeve

An essential element to your authentic success posture is a personal commitment to integrity. Without honesty and uprightness, no success will last. Take out an Integrity Policy on yourself. Many things can change the landscape of your success, but if your integrity remains intact, you will always walk with a posture of authentic success. Dr. Jim Reeve says it best, "It's not how high you jump, it's how straight you walk when you hit the ground. That's the bottom line of success."

CHAPTER 10

Holding the Energy Charge

I t had been a while since I had taken my Harley Davidson motorcycle out for a ride. So last Saturday, I suited up in expectation of getting out on the highway. Throwing the ignition switch, I was greeted with the groaning sound of a starter motor that wasn't receiving the necessary 'oomph' from the battery. The engine cranked over a few times but the power from the electrical system wasn't enough to explode the compressed fuel vapors in the cylinders. The engine didn't come to life and my expectations for a ride died on the spot.

The time that I was supposed to be freewheeling down the highway with a helmet on, was thus spent in my driveway with my mechanic's hat on.

Consulting the owner's manual, I determined that the motorcycle battery could be 'jump started' by another twelve volt battery. So borrowing some electrical juice from my car, I was able to get the motorcycle running. From my past experiences, I knew that jump starting an engine would be a short lived blessing if the battery was not capable of holding the charge it was now receiving from the running engine. The best way to find out was to go for that ride.

> In the right conditions, many can be charged up. But the key to living effective lives is to be able to 'hold the charge' once outside the right conditions.

Sure enough, after the trip, the battery showed no sign of improvement. It was apparent that the battery was not capable of maintaining the charge. The solution? I could either keep giving the motorcycle a jump start every time I wanted some two-wheeled action, or else get a new battery. One that could hold a charge.

People are the same as vehicle batteries. They are either capable of holding a charge or they are constantly in need of getting a jump start. In other words, they are able to motivate themselves to get the job done, or they need someone else to help them get up and going.

As a motivational speaker, I have spent years persuading people to make positive changes. In effect, I go from place to place with a set of mental 'jumper cables'. If anyone is running low on personal power, I do my best to re-energize them and head them in the right direction. I know that an apt word in season can increase a person's harvest forever. I know that a one hour talk can produce a lifetime of results. The motivational message is a powerful tool in affecting change. But I also know its limitations.

While a room full of people can be changed in a moment, I am realistic about the extent of the change. Most can be positively impacted for that moment, fewer are able to translate the effect of that moment into something that lasts. In the right conditions, many can be charged up. But the key to living effective lives is to be able to 'hold the charge' once outside the right conditions. It is easy to make positive decisions in an inspirational environment. But your character is seen in whether you can maintain a commitment to the decisions once you leave the inspiring environment.

Many people profess to being charged up by a speech, meeting, seminar or convention.

But weeks and months down the track, is there any trace of that charge still within them? They received the charge, but could they hold it? Can they retain the energy of what was fed through the jumper cables into the engine compartment of their lives? While there will always be some energy dissipation after the 'event', those who can retain the charge the longest will be the ones that influence the future to their favor.

What does it take to increase your ability to hold a charge? Sometimes all it takes is the power of one presentation or counseling session. Sometimes it comes as a result of long term training and mentorship. Ultimately, it takes the combination of both inspiration and education.

Bayless Conley is one of the world's leading people trainers. While having dinner with him recently, he told me this great analogy: A motivational speaker is like a professional lumberjack. He comes into a country town armed with an array of impressive chainsaws and tree felling devices. With news of the lumberjack's special appearance, the townsfolk turn out to watch the spectacle. After selecting the perfect tree, the lumberjack sets about doing that for which he is skilled. The crowd gasps as he wields his chainsaw prowess before them. The rattling noise of the chainsaw's teeth rip into the flesh of the tree. The lumberjack cuts the trunk with an ease that impresses all those who watch. With the spectacle of sparks and wood chips flying in all directions, the townsfolk are thrilled.

Eventually, the tree starts to lean. Then, with a few loud cracks, the immense tree comes crashing down. It lands with an almighty thump in the exact place that the lumberjack had planned.

> "Okay, you make furniture out if it!"

As the cloud of dust and people's excitement settles, the lumberjack repacks his equipment. Blowing the dust off himself as he has done so a thousand times before, he picks up his chainsaws and heads off to the next town. Just as he makes his way through the admiring crowd, he turns to the town carpenter and says, "Okay, you make furniture out if it!"

We live in a culture that idolizes the lumberjack. Special attention is given to the person who is entertaining and compelling in what they do. The lumberjack can get maximum impact from 'one session'. No doubt, the lumberjack plays a significant role in the scheme of life. Yet the carpenter plays an equally important role. He is the one that takes what the lumberjack hands him and methodically works it to produce something of lasting value.

If you want to increase your ability to hold a charge, then you need the influence of both the lumberjack and the carpenter; someone who can inspire you in a single session and someone who can educate you over time. If you want to help others to hold a charge, ensure that they have both inspiration and education. Here are some ways to maintain your energy charge.

1) You can hold a charge when you are held by your vision.

Bob Taylor dreamed of making guitars. Today, Taylor Guitars is the premier maker of acoustic guitars in the world. Some time ago, I took a tour of the company headquarters. Situated in a glass cabinet in their showroom was a special guitar. To anyone's eye, it looks an exquisite musical instrument replete with intricate mother of pearl inlays on the fret board. But instead of the inlays being the usual guitar artistry, the mother of pearl inlay was placed to form the picture of a forklift!

Back in 1995, Bob Taylor saw a timber shipping pallet lying abandoned behind his manufacturing building. He made the determination to turn the ignoble wood pallet into a beautiful guitar. To the amazement of onlookers, he did so. The making of his Pallet Guitar was for fun and to prove a point: That it is the design and the builder, and not the wood, that define a great guitar. Bob is an example to the truth that greatness is more about the person and his vision rather than having the right elements in place.

The day after Bob started working on his 'pallet guitar', his wife didn't have to say, 'Bob, get out of bed. Go down to the shop and keep working on your guitar.' He didn't need to be jump started. He did not need to be reminded. He did not lose the project in the abyss called 'Someday I'll'. His vision for what the project would achieve kept him charged and on task.

> **Greatness is more about the person and his vision rather than having the right elements in place.**
>
> Bob Taylor

Everyone else saw a shipping device used by forklifts to move heavy loads. When he looked at that pallet, he saw it differently. Bob Taylor saw a beautiful guitar and worked methodically to bring it into reality. Having a strong and sustained vision for what you want to accomplish will help you hold the charge.

2) You can hold a charge when you learn to be comfortable with being uncomfortable.

Having a clear vision is vital, but it's not enough. Too many people abandon their vision when they get their first splinter. Others tolerate many splinters but give up at their first laceration. The fact is that any advancement will require you to be uncomfortable and be uncomfortable for a long time. How long is that, you may ask? Whatever time you initially think it's going to take, triple it. How uncomfortable is it going to be? However hard you initially think it may be, quadruple it. If it turns out to be any less than that, consider yourself lucky! With every advancement, there is a barrier to entry. The only ones to get the reward are the ones who are tough enough to get through the barrier.

> Having a strong connection between comfort and happiness makes you vulnerable to giving up.

Where does a person get this toughness? It simply comes from learning to be comfortable with being uncomfortable. Does this mean that in order to advance to the next level you have to live an uncomfortable life? Yes, but only in the beginning until your senses adjust. Growth is painful because it demands that we snap some moorings which have served us to this point but have no place in our new world. It comes down to snap them or they trap us.

> **If you can be silent and let them do the talking, their life history will reveal patterns.**

Most people endure discomfort in the hope that it will be short-lived. They 'hang in there' hoping for a quick breakthrough so they can be happy again. But having a strong connection between comfort and happiness makes you vulnerable to giving up. It is a debilitating connection that stymies any significant advancement in life. Growth becomes undesirable because you become miserable in the midst of discomfort.

The great thing about the quest for advancement is that it matures you. It asks you to find a more substantial basis for your happiness than comfort. There is nothing like undesirable conditions to cause your spirit to earnestly search for the better foundations for joy. So when the landscape does change for the better; when you finally breakthrough the 'barrier to entry';

when you finally get to that next level; when some comfort returns, you are happy but your happiness hasn't depended on these things.

People who get comfortable with being uncomfortable have the ability to keep 'showing up' regardless of how they feel or how inhospitable their current conditions. They hold a charge because they are energized by the benefits of commitment rather than being energized by comfort.

3) You can hold a charge when you value the 'pattern' reputation of your life.

Ask a person about their past and from it you can likely gauge their future. Unless a person undergoes radical transformation, the pattern of their past will often carry forward to be the pattern of their future. That's why a bank, when assessing someone for a bank loan, will look at their financial pattern. The bank's judgment of your financial character is not so much on how much you earn but on your past financial behavior. You can have a tidy sum in the bank, but they are more interested in how you got it. Was it the result of consistent savings or were you the recipient of a gift?

Suffice to say, the bank will be more inclined to give you a loan if you have established a pattern of being able to save money. Their logic is that if you have the discipline to save, then it is likely that you will have the discipline to make loan repayments. If you have a big sum of money as a result of a gift, this is no evidence to a bank manager that you're able to handle the responsibility of repayments. In assessing you for a loan, the banks place a high value on your long-term financial pattern. They are not going to loan you money based on you having a New Year's resolution to pay it back!

> One of the strongest testimonies to your character is a pattern of consistency to your life.

A person's pattern of life is a defining element to their advancement or lack thereof. Brian Houston, founder of the hugely successful Hillsong organization says, "The strongest [organizations] are the ones who consistently follow their course." Individually or as an organization, to consistently follow your course requires the skill of maintaining your charge through thick and a lot of thin!

Whenever someone comes to you with a 'great idea', the place to start your evaluation is not with the idea but with them. Find out about their history. If you can be silent and let them do the talking, their life history will reveal patterns.

These patterns will usually validate their ideas or discredit them.

To advance requires the help of others. Specifically help from those who are at the place you want to be. In turn, they will evaluate your candidacy for help based on the patterns of your life. The last thing you want is a history of jumping around from one place to another. That gives an impression that your ability to hold a charge is limited.

> **They are not going to loan you money based on you having a New Year's resolution to pay it back!**

One of the strongest testimonies to your character is a pattern of consistency to your life. If you can develop the ability to hold a charge without depending on the 'right conditions' in order to do so, you build consistency into your life. It will raise your value in the eyes of others and give you more credibility. As the following graph shows, enthusiasm and consistency will increase people's opinion of you. And as their opinion of you increases, so will the opportunities for advancement.

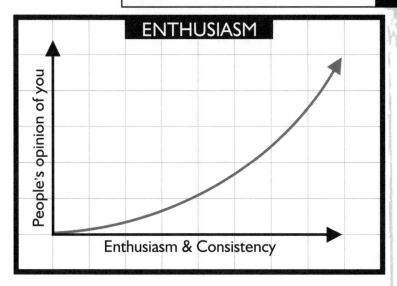

If you want to advance in your life but are unsure of the direction that you should head, heed this advice: Be of value, where you are, right now. Resist being inconsistent. There may be times in your life when you need to change from one thing to another, but doing this too often establishes inconsistency into your history. This adversely affects your future. Great opportunities don't naturally flow to the inconsistent. Of all the things for which you can be known, be known as one who can hold a charge.

4) You can hold a charge when you are disciplined about replenishment.

Sometimes, a car battery will struggle to hold a charge because it is low on electrolyte (water). If the battery is not irreparably damaged, it can be restored to charge holding capability by adding the needed fluid and receiving a jump start. People are the same way. There will be times in your pursuit of a better life when you struggle to get motivated. You are drained and in need of some form of inspirational electrolyte. This comes in many forms: rest, vacation, counseling, books, teaching, conferences, travel. It is your responsibility to recognize when you need an inspirational 'top up' and a jump start.

When it comes to other people holding a charge, we do well to recognize that some people live from jump start to jump start. They never actually want to hold the charge. They are not disciplined and don't replenish their electrolyte. When the need becomes obvious, they like getting a boost of energy from you or any other good natured soul! You can save yourself a lot of heartbreak and frustration by being quick to recognize those who are just low on a little electrolyte and those who have no intention of

> **Don't lower the standard of your life or organization to accommodate individuals who lack commitment.**

ever holding their own charge. You certainly can't build a team or a friendship out of the latter.

I value the wisdom of T.D. Jakes on this subject: "More times than not we use our optimism or persuasive style to coerce others into accepting our goals and objectives. But they cannot run off your fuel, nor can they become something just because you believe that they can. They must possess their own faith for the many challenges that are always along the way to accomplishment. It is often a bad sign if you have to jump start them every day. Like a car with a dry cell in its battery, if they do not hold a charge, it may be a sign of a deeper trouble. You must remember that anyone you have to keep motivating to get started, you may have to motivate to maintain."

5) You can hold a charge when you commit excellence to menial tasks.

If someone wants an esteemed position in my organization, I will always start them out with a lesser task. Something that is menial and low on the glamour scale. It is the ultimate way of testing a person's depth of character. I have come to learn that some people want to be lumberjacks right out of the box. Having made the mistake of giving lumberjack positions to people before I determined their ability to hold a charge, has made me wiser.

These days I look for people who can see the potential in an old wooden pallet and enthusiastically turn it into something useful. There are a lot of people out there with that excellent carpenter spirit. They are less enamored by being admired and more enamored by building something for future generations. I am blessed to have many of them in my team. Some of them are growing into world class lumberjacks!

Don't lower the standard of your life or organization to accommodate individuals who lack commitment. Better to cut them loose, even if it initially hurts you. It's never to your detriment to cut off that which refuses to heal. By doing so, you make room for people who can raise the quality of life by their excellence and reliability.

CHAPTER 11

From Individual Success to Team Success

Relationships are always more important than accomplishments. But to combine relationships with accomplishments is an awesome way to experience the best of both worlds. Personal success is better than personal non-development, but team success is the ultimate success.

When you are starting out in life, climbing up into the saddle of your own horse is task enough. You concentrate hard on survival. Once you have conquered that you come to a realization that there's more to life than being a successful Lone Ranger. Indeed, you sense the reason why you have succeeded. You can help others learn to ride, so that you can ride places together.

The natural order of advancement is for an

individual success to eventually manifest itself into team success. There comes a time when any further personal success can only be developed in the context of community. As a conclusion to a psychology study, Dr. David Niven wrote: "People who acknowledge the interdependent nature of life, the importance of human connections and our collective existence, were twice as likely to consider themselves successful as those who held completely individualistic views." Leading a team to succeed will advance your life beyond what you can do by yourself. And to Niven's point, collective advancement will cause you to feel more success-ful than you would from a solo advance.

> **Leading a team to succeed will advance your life beyond what you can do by yourself.**

There is something intrinsic to human nature that makes succeeding more meaningful in the context of a team. Harvard political scientist, Robert D. Putnam, identifies what he believes is a central crisis of our time; the decline in group activity. In his book, *Bowling Alone*, Putnam urges folks to get out from behind their computer screens and join a people group. Individualism,

Putnam says, is making us less happy, less healthy and less wise.

There is a greater enjoyment and a heightened sense of success that can only be experienced within a team context. Group advancement does make us happier, healthier and wiser. As someone aptly said, "Success is sweeter with others, and failure is easier if you're with others."

While going from individual success to team success has its benefits, it also introduces you to a whole new range of challenges. Sometimes you will long for the simpler days, when you only had yourself to worry about. Any time you bring people into an equation, things get more complex.

> There is a level of personal advancement that can only be achieved when you take the plunge into leadership.

A few years ago, some friends invited us to go camping. We thought we had packed everything needed, but realized that we didn't bring enough firewood. As the night closed in, the temperature dropped to the point where the campfire was no longer for creating atmosphere but essential to avoiding hypothermia!

Searching the surrounding forest for firewood was to no avail. In the absence of an axe and three hours of daylight, the best I could do was find a bunch of dried pine cones. I threw a few cones onto the fire and discovered that the dry pine cone was a satisfactory alternative fuel.

> Some of the best leaders are those who didn't give up when they discovered that they weren't born leaders.

So after several trips into the forest, I procured enough pine cones to keep the campfire blazing for hours. The only drawback was that by the end of the night, I was covered in pine cone sap. I dare not have hugged anyone goodnight lest they would stick to me like superglue!

Leading a team will save you from the hypothermia of personal isolation. There is a warming to the human spirit that can only take place in the team context. But leading a team also means that, from time to time, things get sticky. And this is why many capable people resist the natural progression to go into team leadership. In a sense, you are inviting extra challenges into your life. And given our desire to keep life as simple as possible, we avoid extra challenges, especially if they're more optional in nature.

Can you be successful and never lead a team? Absolutely. But there is a level of personal advancement that can only be achieved when you take the plunge into leadership. Though the plunge will introduce some new challenges, they are ultimately good for you. The key is not to avoid leadership but to acquire the skills, wisdom and perseverance to lead a vibrant team amidst the occasional stickiness that comes with it.

Building a Team

People take longer to meld than banging two bits of wood together. For any team or organization to create a culture and sustain it takes time. People need time to understand, assimilate and be committed to that culture. Time is the great refiner. Time affords you the opportunity to realize your personality deficiencies, such as the need to please, and gives you the opportunity to deal with them. Time sorts out those who are meant to be on your team and those who are not meant to be on your team.

Unless you catch a providential wave of momentum, you will find that team building starts slowly. It takes longer than you hoped it would. Frustratingly longer. But there are some benefits. As someone once said, "One of the key benefits to starting out small is that you can learn from your mistakes anonymously!"

Don't be too quick to buy into the notion of being a 'born leader'. In reality, most leaders are cultivated. Perhaps this is the reason why many potential leaders never lead a team. They tried it once, dipped their finger in, but pulled back when they experienced the first touch of stickiness. They concluded from their initial experience that they must not be 'cut out to be a leader'. So they withdraw from the leadership field and focus on their own affairs. They can still lead effective lives but not as effective as they would have been if they had pushed through the stickiness. Some of the best leaders are those who didn't give up when they discovered that they weren't born leaders. Instead, they studied, discovered and incorporated the missing ingredients and became cultivated leaders.

Setting Yourself Up for Some Criticism

In the movie, *The Godfather II*, Al Pacino's character, Michael Corleone, shares his father's advice to "keep your friends close, but your enemies closer." Hearing these sentiments for the first time, I thought, I don't have any enemies. I was living life as nicely as possible, being careful not to offend anyone. For the life of me, I couldn't think of one person who knew me personally that would have considered me an enemy.

However, since taking the reins of leadership of my own organization, I can vouch for having quite a few people displeased with me. Not that becoming a leader turned me into an enemy producing tyrant such as Vito or Michael Corleone. But I have come to realize that when you take the reins of leadership, you make

> ## Toughen your hide but don't harden your heart.
>
> Vance Havner

yourself vulnerable to criticism. What's worse is that many times you deserve it!

A leader is a positive example for other people to follow. But sometimes, especially early in your leadership, you don't quite get it right. In fact, you can get it quite wrong. Lacking experience and perfection, you make some mistakes. Now when your advancement is an individual pursuit, generally you alone wear the consequences of your mistake. But when you are building a team, your mistakes involve and impact the lives of other people. The consequences of such is that your mistakes can hurt people and they don't ap-preciate you for it. Needless to say, it's a humbling experience. At this point, some abdicate their leadership and return to a former life. But if you receive the lesson and keep moving forward, you recover. If a lack of leadership wisdom got you into the stickiness, pushing through it will cause you to emerge with whatever wisdom you lacked.

While making a few leadership mistakes can foist criticism upon you, sometimes you are targeted just because you are the leader. You may have done nothing to deserve the criticism. Kevin Wilcock, an effective team leader in Australia, counsels leaders not to take it personally. In his words: "People can be unusual creatures of habit and will blame whatever circumstance on the highest person in authority that they know." Don't automatically assume that your leadership is at fault. Sometimes you are receiving the criticism by virtue of the position that you hold rather than anything that you have done.

Then, there is the situation where you make the right leadership decision but it conflicts with someone's expectations. They get hurt and let you know by an insult of their choosing. That's why the late, great Vance Havner said, "A leader ought to have the mind of a scholar, the heart of a child and the hide of a rhinoceros. But as you toughen your hide, see to it that you don't harden your heart." Leading a team to success is awesome but you will have to deal with some occasional stickiness. Be a good leader by navigating the foibles of team building. And remember Vance Havner's advice to toughen your hide but don't harden your heart.

When Someone Quits Your Team

Simon McIntyre has helped to build over one hundred organizations around the world. I first met Simon in 1985 when he had only one organization in existence. During our conversation, he said something that has stayed with me over the years. In relating

> A good leader is one who can 'keep trucking' in leadership when people are coming and going all the time!

some of his leadership experiences, he made the comment, "Not everyone who starts with you, will stay with you." He briefed me on their history. Of all the people who were a part of their organization at the beginning, only a 'rock solid few' were still with them five years later.

Over the years, I fell into the trap of thinking a good leader should be able to retain everyone. The reality is that a good leader is one who can 'keep trucking' in leadership when people are coming and going all the time! People join teams and leave teams for all types of reasons. Here are some of the major reasons why people join your team and then later, un-join your team!

#1 People's Availability

People's availability to join you in the first place should be your first signal. It is one thing if they have just moved into the area or they are at a legitimate crossroads in their life. But some people come to you because they became negative about their previous post in life. As a team builder, how should you respond? Welcome everyone. You don't need to sort them out. The culture of your team and time will sort out the legitimate team members from the bullfrogs and butterflies.

#2 The Victim in Need of a Villain

As I outlined in chapter five, there are some people who have a victim mentality woven into the fabric of their identity. They will be with you until you challenge them to get better. You doing so makes it very hot for them but they know they can't leave the kitchen without a 'legitimate reason'. So they inevitably villainize the cook. In that way, their leaving is not their fault, it's yours. It justifies their departure.

Don't be surprised if the victim calls a few of your team members and warns them about your bad cooking!

#3 The Quit Virus

Some people have a quit virus in their blood stream. Even if the team that they are on is doing wonders for their life and future, they still quit. It's a habit. It's the one thing in life that they're really good at—starting but not finishing. There is no cure for such a virus. It is contagious. Make sure they don't infect you on their way out!

#4 Looking for a Savior

Some people spend their lives searching for a savior. The one who is going to wave the magic wand and make life perfect for them. You might just be the next guru on their long list. They will join your team in the hope that you will turn their water into wine. When you are unable to perform the miracle, they will stay with you for a while until they hear about Guru X working wonders across the other side of town. What should you do? Let them go with your best guru blessing!

#5 Spotlight Seekers

If your team has become noticeable, be prepared

for some spotlight seekers. These are people who want to share in the glory of someone else's success. They will chase it and do everything they can to wriggle their way into the existing spotlight. Their desire is to get a slice of that glory. What they don't understand is that there is no satisfaction in borrowed glory.

A spotlight seeker, also known as a 'Johnny Come Lately', doesn't realize that by the time something is successful, all the great spotlight positions have been awarded to those who were committed from the beginning. Those, who with sweat and tears sacrificed to create something noticeable out of years of unnoticed development, are the ones who get the good positions. Spotlight seekers need to learn that, instead of jumping from team to team, instead of trying to jockey and jive into existing success, if they settled down and used their energy to build their team, the spotlight would eventually find them.

#6 The Empty Oven

There is a saying: If you put out a menu, make sure there is something cooking in the oven. Sometimes people will leave your team because they discover what you have in the oven is not enough for them. When your team or organization is starting out, you are not going to be able to offer everything. Be prepared for wonderful people to check out your team for a little while but then leave.

When you set your disappointment aside, you'll understand why. It's not that they didn't like what they saw, it just wasn't enough for them. What they were looking for was just plainly beyond your capabilities. Rather than become despondent, be grateful that they were with you for a little while.

It is quite possible that for the time they were with you, they added something good to make your team a little stronger.

It takes a while for your team to build an oven big enough to be filled with every type of

> People 'self-select' themselves in and out of your organization. All you need to do is maintain your vision and stay true to your culture.

treat. Until then, just make sure that you have something in the oven that is nourishing and the result of your best effort.

Gains and Losses

Get acclimatized to the fact that you will have people leave your team. Even when your team or organization reaches that critical mass, you will still have to live with the loss of a few great people here and there. Some will leave for the reasons outlined above, others for different reasons. Psychologist Dr. Phillip McGraw says, "No matter how flat the pancake—it still has two sides." You will only know with certainty the details from your side. So make sure your side is the best it can be.

Keep in mind that some subtractions from your team can be beneficial. Every team has a culture and if a person is at loggerheads with your culture, they won't be an effective team member. The good news is that you don't have to remove them. They will remove themselves. On the whole, people 'self-select' themselves in and out of your organization. All you need to do is maintain your vision and stay true to your culture. Those that do fit will stay. Those that don't fit will move on. Resist the inclination to take the loss personally.

Realize that every leader has to learn to live with abandonment. Even the best leaders in the world have had people leave their team. A team of people is not static. The tide will ebb and flow as people move in and out of your team. The key is to love them while you have them but hold them loosely.

CHAPTER 12

Grow Your Team's Success

Coming together is a beginning, staying together is progress, and working together is success.

—Henry Ford

History shows that it takes a lot more to galvanize people into a team than a few weeks. Business studies have shown that it takes seven years for a new business to grow through all the critical phases to maturity. In building a team, you need to adjust your mind for the long haul. Too many people embark on an endeavor tuned for a four hundred meter run when they should have tuned their mind for a four hundred mile run. Sometimes our supporters, in their enthusiasm, influence us to tune our minds towards only having to run a short distance to succeed. Then, when we find ourselves having to run much further than that, we can become demoralized. Better to tune your mind for the long run and be pleasantly surprised when you see victory sooner.

Understand that just as people do not grow at the same rate, neither do teams and organizations grow at the same rate. One of the traps that leaders fall into is comparing their results with the results of other leaders. It's a no-win situation. If someone else seems to be getting better results than you, there is the propensity for you to get discouraged. Conversely, if you compare yourself to someone who is not doing as well as you, then you could be feeding your pride. Discouragement and pride are both energy sapping diversions. By all means, be inspired by others and learn from them, but steer clear of the perilous territory of comparison.

> Better to tune your mind for the long run and be pleasantly surprised when you see victory sooner.

There is a lot about our progression which we can control. For example, the decision to advance is in our control. The direction of our advancement is in our control. The timing of our start is in our control. But when it comes to the rate of advancement, this is largely beyond our control. Patience and perseverance, two under sensationalized virtues, are often trod under foot in our quest to want to grow fast. My own brother, Chris Beavis, offers this valuable advice: "Don't put your baby on steroids because you want it to grow faster. The result will be freakish."

Stories of freakish growth often get attention because they are fascinating aberrations of what is normal. So one of the fundamental questions you need to ask yourself is, 'Why you do I want fast growth?' There is every possibility that you want it for the wrong reasons: the attention, the accolades, the excitement, the acceptance by peers. Perhaps you want fast growth to avoid the tedium and testing of the slow natural growth. What is best for your team members? What is best for your team is for you to have the time to personally invest in their lives, helping them to understand the vision and adapt to the culture. You can't do this when your growth is explosive. Remember too, that gangbuster growth can just as readily become gangbuster loss.

If you want to build a team of quality people, it will take time. Because quality people don't hand their trust over without scrutiny. The only way to gain this trust is to give them the time to realize your authenticity. When your team members sense that they know your heart, it paves the way for them to pledge their loyalty. Leadership trainer, Dan Reiland, says, "People won't follow those they don't trust. They won't trust those with

> Your goal is not to build a perfect team, but a healthy one.

whom they don't connect. And they won't connect with you if they can't find your heart." Gaining the trust of quality people takes longer, sometimes years. And they are every bit worth the wait.

Build the Capabilities of Your People

If you are going to the effort of building a team, then build it strong. I have seen organizations burst on to the scene with breathtaking pace only to have them burst off the scene at an even faster pace. When you examine the carnage and sift through the wreckage, you inevitably find the lack of a substantial foundation. You can't build a fire with rotten wood. When it comes to the strength of your team, it is not necessarily how capable you are, but rather how you build the capabilities of your people.

Your goal is not to build a perfect team, but a healthy one. Health is the best goal because healthy things grow. Teach your team to value service. Team members that serve the vision of the team, rather than their own agendas, make the team healthy.

Bono, the lead singer of the band U2, was asked why his band was able to stay together and achieve longevity. His answer was that as individuals they denied their egos but collectively, as a band, they had a big ego. The health of any team depends on the same: Personal egos are set aside for the sake of what is best for the team.

Every vital position in your team must be filled with someone who is secure enough to set their own agendas aside and do what is best for the team. Too many organizations give vital positions to insecure people because they have the ability to perform. Insecure people can often perform but they are unable to serve. Any organization with insecure people in key positions is unhealthy and will not grow. It is better to give a

> They have to see the vision work in you first, before they buy into it themselves.

vital position to someone who can serve, even if they may not be able to do the job quite as proficiently as the 'insecure performer'.

Qualities of a Great Team Leader

Give your team members a way to follow you. If you don't, you frustrate them. All they can do is admire you, envy you, be intimidated by you, or worse, criticize you. You cannot get behind your team members and push them. Remember that leadership is being a positive example that others can follow. You have to lead your team by example. Your life has to be the proof of the pudding. They have to see the vision work in you first, before they buy into it themselves.

> Your role as a leader is to absorb uncertainty.

A great leader loves to see the influence of their team members increase. The mark of an insecure leader is seen in their reticence to see their team members gain influence. They fear their value will decrease if someone else's value increases. If an excelling team member is loyal, then endorse them. Doing so increases their value even more. If they are showing signs of disloyalty to the team, remove them. Rob Koke, leader of a large organization in

Texas, tells us how: "If you have team members with whom your spirit tolerates but no longer endorses, remove them graciously, generously and swiftly!" The longer you wait to make a tough call, the tougher it gets.

A great leader doesn't inflict a roller coaster ride upon his organization. In fact, your role as a leader is to absorb uncertainty. If you or your team are going through trying times, don't draw their attention to what you are going through but rather draw their attention to where you are going to. Get their eyes off the ground and onto the horizon.

A wise leader doesn't reassure too much because this will raise suspicions that you are trying to conceal your uncertainty with the same reassurance. A leader learns what it takes to keep his team up when personally he is down. Ultimately, a great leader has the resolve of Christopher Columbus, who during days of despair, uncertainty and the threat of mutiny, would write in his log: "This day we sailed on!"

The Joy of Being a Leader

Can you be successful and never lead a team? Sure. But there is a level of personal success that can only be achieved by leading a team to succeed. Leading a team draws out the best in you. Leading a team grinds out the worst in you. Leading a team is one of the most fulfilling, heart-warming experiences of life, despite having to deal with a little stickiness from time to time. The bold truth is that everyone has the potential to be a leader. It is our opportunity to make our lives count more fully in the lives of others.

Leading a team enables us to not only experience the joy of advancement in our own lives, but we have the privilege of celebrating the advancements of our team members. There is great joy in seeing others reap the benefits of success. You have reached the upper echelons of success when you enjoy the victories of your team even more than your own.

One of the saddest sentences in the whole Bible was written about a leader who totally missed the point of leadership. The life of Jehoram, King of Judah was summed up with this succinct record: "He passed away to no one's regret." His legacy brings to light the words of the late Dr. Norman Vincent Peale: "The man who lives for himself is a failure; the man who lives for others has achieved true success."

CHAPTER 13

The Key to Future Increase

U nlike other makeovers, the success makeover is not a one time event. It is the ongoing process of advancing by improvement. Success and the key to future increase is *finishing today having improved on yesterday and doing the same tomorrow.*

Yes, success is hard. The natural gravitational energy of life is to pull you backwards not push you forwards. If you are going to move forward, it has to be a result of you overriding the natural order of things. Success isn't going to track you down and force itself upon you. But mediocrity will. It's easy to stay the same. Even easier to slip backwards. All you have to do is go with the flow. But if you want to succeed, you fight the flow;

you push against it; you overcome it, and you do it daily. You make the decision that however you finished yesterday, be it dismal or victorious, today will be an improvement on it.

Improving on Your Good Times

Several years ago, I was involved in the leadership of an organization. There were hundreds of people involved and it was a lot of fun. In my last year with them, I was traveling to speaking engagements so frequently that I sensed it was time for me to hand over the reins of leadership. It was a tough decision. I was very fond of the people in my team and had created many memories while there. I resigned and moved on, or so I thought. Four months after leaving the organization physically, I was in a taxi on the other side of the globe. It was then that I left the organization mentally.

> Success isn't going to track you down and force itself upon you.

It had been cold when I departed from Los Angeles. I was wearing a jacket that had the corporate insignia of the organization from which I had resigned. It was my favorite jacket. It fit well and the insignia was the stylistic product of my design team. It had sentimental value and apart from that, it was an expensive jacket!

Upon arriving in Sydney, the heat reminded me that during my sixteen hour flight I had switched seasons from winter to summer. Getting into the taxi was my opportunity to take my jacket off. When the taxi arrived at my destination in the

> If yesterday was good, honor it by not allowing it to hold you back from making today even better.

city, I helped the driver get my baggage from the trunk, or the boot as they say in Australia.

As the taxi drove off, I realized that I had left my favorite jacket in the back seat. My immediate reaction was to call the taxi company headquarters and inform them that I had left something valuable in the back seat. I was sure that prompt action would get the jacket back. But then I heard the voice: "Wes, leave it in the taxi. That jacket does not represent your future. Let that era of your life go. Something new awaits you. It's time to get on with what's ahead." I don't know if it was the voice of God or the spirit of Og Mandino, maybe both. What I did know was that the voice was right. My job was to improve on yesterday, not hold onto it.

No matter how good life has become, there is always a better tomorrow out there somewhere. If we let the successes of our past be a springboard, instead of an anchor, then we won't be held back from discovering those better days. If yesterday was good, honor it by not allowing it to hold you back from making today even better.

Improving on Your Tough Times

One fateful Saturday in 2003, Americans awoke to the news that the space shuttle Columbia broke up during re-entry into the earth's atmosphere. Supporters of space exploration and citizens of humanity all over the world, spent the day stunned by the vast loss. Every television network canceled regular programming to cover the press conference with Milt Heflin, Chief Flight Director, and Ron Dittemore, Shuttle Program Manager.

> "When we have a bad day, we work to fix it."
>
> Space shuttle Columbia Chief Flight Director, Milt Heflin

No one knew exactly what the events were that contributed to the tragedy. Explanations were mere conjecture at that point. Heflin and Dittemore had to grapple not only with the devastating failure of a mission, but with the reality that those who perished were their friends. As I watched these men speak to the nations, they may have been at a loss for some answers but they were not at a loss for resolve. All the exemplary qualities of strong leadership emerged from their demeanor as they fielded questions.

In responding to what was one of the lowest points in NASA's history, Chief Flight Director, Milt Heflin, said, "When we have a bad day, we work to fix it." In responding to how they were going to deal with the loss, Shuttle Program Manager, Ron Dittemore, said, "The best therapy in this business is to get on with your job."

We would do well to follow their lead. If yesterday was tough, our job today is to start our comeback. It's the best therapy out there. What's

> If your house is burning down and you are combating the fire with your garden hose, a change of attitude or making a greater effort is not going to help.

more, it is a therapy which produces favorable

results. As the Psalm states: "Those who sow in tears, will reap in joy." We can't change the events of yesterday, but we can make tomorrow's harvest better by sowing the seeds of improvement today.

Improving Your Ability

English novelist, Phyllis Bottome, wrote: "There are two ways of meeting difficulties: You alter the difficulties, or you alter yourself meeting them." Often, we can alter our difficulties with a change in attitude or some hard work. But this may not always be the solution. If your house is burning down and you are combating the fire with your garden hose, a change of attitude or making a greater effort is not going to help. Likewise, when tackling the fires of life, attitude and effort is extremely important. But there are situations when we have to admit our need to expand the size of our hose.

In the book, *The 100 Simple Secrets of Successful People*, Dr. David Niven says, "Effort, by itself, is a terrible predictor of outcomes. Because inefficient effort is a tremendous source of discouragement. It leaves people to conclude that they can never succeed since even expending maximum effort has not produced results." There is more to advancing than just having a heart for it. There will be times when our talent has to catch up with our heart.

John C. Maxwell addresses this by saying, "A dream is not enough. If your abilities do not match your dream then it will be a nightmare. If you don't have the aptitude or the skill level to do it, you're going to have some real frustrations." If your quest for advancement is being frustrated, it's likely that the solution lies in increasing your skill.

The merits of vision, the right attitude, working hard and persevering are not enough. Without the development of your skill set, these merits will just get you to the point of failure quicker. Your intelligence quotient is not set in concrete. What is to stop you from increasing it? The development of your skills in combination with your vision, attitude, hard work and perseverance is a powerful life improvement combination.

> There will be times when our talent has to catch up with our heart.

Finishing a Winner

Since 1948, Bud Greenspan has been covering the Olympics as a broadcaster, journalist and filmmaker. This award winning, sports producer and historian has captured the great moments in Olympic history. Moments often missed by a culture that only acknowledges those who stand on the victory podium. Of all the victors he has seen in Olympic glory, one of his heroes is John Stephen Akhwari.

John Stephen Akhwari represented Tanzania at the 1968 Olympics, held in Mexico City. He was a marathon runner. As the signal started the race, Akhwari ran with all the might of one who had dreams of winning a gold medal. But a few miles into the race, he was involved in an accident. His quest for a medal had ended, yet he continued to run. With his right leg bandaged, Tanzania's John Stephen Akhwari entered the stadium more than an hour after the winners had finished the marathon race. Only a few hundred spectators remained in the stadium.

> "You're bloodied and in great pain. Why did you do this?"

Though Akhwari was running as best he could, he was running only to finish in last place. In great pain, both physically and emotionally, Akhwari hobbled around the darkened track to complete his run. Bud Greenspan went to him and asked the question: "You're bloodied and in great pain. Why did you do this?" In Greenspan's mind, it would have made perfect sense for Akhwari to pull out of the race at the point of sustaining the injury. In response to Greenspan's question, Akhwari said, "My country did not send me five thousand miles to start the race. My country sent me here to finish it!"

Those powerful words from John Stephen Akhwari apply to every man and woman. We are all in the race of life. Regardless of how we started the race, whether we were favored to win or whether we have fallen behind, the choice of how we will finish is up to us. It doesn't matter if you have botched the run so far. It doesn't

> "My country did not send me five thousand miles to start the race. My country sent me here to finish it!"
>
> John Stephen Akhwari

matter if you are injured and are running hurt. It doesn't matter if you are not considered a medal contender. It doesn't matter if you're running last. It doesn't matter if darkness has fallen on you. All that matters is whether you will keep running.

Put one foot after the other in the right direction. And if you do, every step forward is an improvement on your position. Keep going and you will win. Because my friends, in this race called life, everyone who doesn't give up, everyone who keeps advancing, will finish a winner.

They say that we make our decisions then our decisions make us. If you make the decision to daily improve your life and the lives of others, your decision will make you a winner. That's the outcome of the success makeover.

-Wes Beavis-